The Journey
Home

A Collection of Poetry

Mike N. Armijo

ISBN 978-1-0980-2376-8 (paperback)
ISBN 978-1-0980-2377-5 (digital)

Copyright © 2020 by Mike N. Armijo

All rights reserved. No part of this publication may be reproduced, distributed, or transmitted in any form or by any means, including photocopying, recording, or other electronic or mechanical methods without the prior written permission of the publisher. For permission requests, solicit the publisher via the address below.

Christian Faith Publishing, Inc.
832 Park Avenue
Meadville, PA 16335
www.christianfaithpublishing.com

Printed in the United States of America

My Constant Provider

HE said not to worry of what we will wear or what we will eat;
that HE would provide everything that we need.
Up until now HE has done what HE said;
for where I am now, HE is looking ahead.
HE is already there to provide what I need;
it is HE who cares and we who HE feeds.
JEHOVAH JIRA, who provides in HIS love;
HE has told us that by faith, HIS grace was enough.
It has not always been easy, for we've all had our days;
we had fear and we doubted, but in faith we still prayed.
We got on our knees as we cried, "Oh GOD, please! hear my plea."
"Take away all which I do not believe."
Our GOD is faithful. HE'S been tried and HE'S true;
when HE hung on that cross, HE did it for you.
The WAY, the TRUTH, our LIGHT from above;
yes, even in fear, HE is faithful in love.
HE only wants what is best for HIS children, you know;
those who love HIM by faith and will not let HIM go.
If we say we love GOD yet hate those around;
we must put it to question—is our love truly sound?
When we feed and we clothe those whose lives are so grim;
the very least of the brethren, we did it for HIM.
The ones dirty and tattered, homeless, in need;
those hungry and broken are the ones we should feed.
Soup and salvation at the foot of the cross;
seeking and serving the hurt and the lost.
There will come a time, when our time will end;
did we make the least of our brothers our friends?
Did we love our sisters and show them the way?

Were we CHRIST-LIKE at the end of the day?
Did we love as HE loves? Made ourselves to be least?
Putting others before or did we do as we pleased?
All praises to HIM who has shown us the way;
as we humbly bow and give thanks as we pray.
The salt and the light of a world gone dim;
by HIS grace we are saved, and it's all due to HIM.
Yes, HE will provide, for HE is faithful and true;
When we call ourselves Christians, it's in the love which we do.
Love is not a meaningless word, by all means;
it is proven with actions and it needs to be seen.
Not out of pride or intentions of self;
saying, "Hey, look what I've done!"
Love is who we become as we follow GOD'S SON.

Fix Your Eyes on Jesus

Fix your eyes on JESUS, you will find compassion there;
have faith as a child does, call out to Call out in prayer.
Be as little children, knowing HE cares.
Fix your heart upon HIM, trust HIM without doubt.
HE is gentle, full of kindness, that's who our LORD's about.
Once HE lives within your heart you'll find, you will not want HIM out.
You too can walk on water as Peter did that day;
have faith like a child and do not look toward the waves.
Fix your eyes upon HIM and trust the ONE to whom you pray.
We all fall short, for all do sin; just know GOD had a plan.
Without the shedding of HIS blood, that sin would always stand.
GOD made a way; call out HIS name, reach out, take HIS hand.
So fix your eyes on JESUS; don't look upon the waves;
walk upon the water, to the ONE who is the WAY.
Like Peter found as he started to sink; it's only GOD who saves.
Fix your mind on JESUS; trust HIM, and obey.
HE took our sin upon HIMSELF on the cross that day.

I Believe

I believe I can walk upon water, above all of life's burdens and pains;
above everything that would cause me to sink in the mire, in that
filth once again.
I believe I can soar as an eagle, high, so majestic and free;
that I can fly above every doubt and all fear, far above everything that
I see.
I believe in the grace which GOD gave me this faith so I know that
I know;
I believe HE will always sustain me, that my soul HE will never let go.
I believe I can walk upon water, so I asked, "May I come out to thee?"
HE said, "Come." So I walked on the waters of life; can't nothing
impossible be.
I believe

Journey Home

Our journey is not over, there is much that we will bear.
There will be tears and happiness, of which we're unaware.
But just remember, look ahead and with each step you trod;
the end is not the end, my friend, for it will lead you to our GOD.
In this world, you will find evil is growing with each day,
GOD said there would be trouble; but HIS truth would light our way.
Hold on to HIS promises, for HIS WORD is right;
be mindful, there's a battlefield, and we must stand and fight.
HE has overcome all things, so we must not quit or sway;
the glory all belongs to HIM, for HE has made a way.
That Way is in HIS SON alone, who hung upon that cross;
to save a world so filled with sin, HE died to save the lost.
We all possess this thing we bear, because of man's first sin;
a hereditary cancer that eats us from within.
HE died for us and suffered, to pay a debt HE did not owe;
but once by faith through saving grace, HE will not let you go.
So on this journey, listen and search with all your heart;
study, show yourself approved; HE finishes what HE starts.
This race we run will end one day, at the end of what is time;
but GOD is on the other side, where eternity we'll find.
A place where sadness will not be, where tears will not be seen;
a place of rest, no sin is found, no wars or suffering.
A home which is not here on earth, prepared for you and me;
our journey is not over, friend; move forward and believe.

Run to God

We see the world's in darkness, its light is growing dim;
seems worse today than yesterday, result of all its sins.
The left side and the right side divided as they are;
political delusions that have gone way too far.
GOD said that man would love himself, we've found it all but true;
where wrong is right and right is wrong, confused in what we do.
Christians persecuted, how hate is now the norm;
the demons know their time is short in this evil storm.
Fake news to bring confusion at every twist and turn;
the world is getting darker and one day, it will burn.
So run to GOD and trust HIM, be children of the day;
the cross was meant to save you, to show you all the way.
The way is found in JESUS, the SAVIOR of mankind;
run to HIM and follow HIM, just leave the world behind.
Believe that it was finished as HE bowed HIS head and died;
salvation for believers who have cast the world aside.
For those who love HIM and obey, repented of their ways;
whose hearts were cold and solid as a lump of hardened clay.
The POTTER now will soften you as you give your life to HIM;
to mold you to perfection, free from darkened sin.
Refined in the fire to make you born again.
So run to GOD, dear children, for HE did not stay dead
HE rose to life to give us life, that is why HE bled.
We are redeemed, HE values what the world just sees as waste;
see that GOD is only good, it only takes a taste.
Abandon this old world, all the bad things that it gives;
for it is like a sinking ship, jump off and you will live.
Run to the arms who loves you, HIS grace will see you through;
have faith in HIM, dear children, on that cross HE thought of you.

Without that shedding of HIS blood, sin would have ruled and reigned;
HE took the strips upon HIS back that should have been our pain.
Run as fast as you can run into our Father's love;
the world and everything it gives could never be enough.

God's Got This

Even this will pass away.
"GOD'S got this," are three words which we should say,
we stand in faith HE'S made a way
to turn our darkness into day.
GOD'S got you, in HIS hands HE holds
your destiny, the truth be told,
for HE knows every tear you cry
and soon in time they will all dry.
"GOD'S got this!" should be our decree
as we bow down on bended knee
by HIS grace He'll see us through;
when HIS blood was shed, HE thought of you.
With just a mustard seed of faith
HE says that mountains can be moved.
GOD'S got the world in HIS hands
HIS will be done as HE commands;
HIS ways are not our ways, you'll see
so trust HIS plan, on HIM believe.
Grace through faith will make a way;
"GOD'S got this too," is what I pray
for life is changing every day.
So as we walk today by faith
believing in HIS saving grace;
knowing HE will make a way
and trusting things will be okay;
let us not doubt but stand in faith.
With all the worries, worldly cares,
which often find us unprepared
to handle things which come our way;

let us repent of doubt and pray.
Yes, *GOD'S got this!*
It's HE who makes a way
by grace through faith you'll be okay.

The Unchanging Word

We praise YOUR holy name, oh GOD our tears have led to YOU;
YOU are the beginning and the end, so faithful and so true.
No matter where we were back then, as we look back in time;
YOU saved us from an awful fate and opened up our eyes.
We are secure in who YOU are, worthy of our praise;
YOU have counted us as YOURs, oh LORD, as YOU know each
  star by name.
Our focus now should be on YOU, without YOU we cannot be;
now it's upon YOUR faithfulness, in humbleness we cleave.
YOU sent your SON who shed HIS blood, who paid a debt HE did
  not owe;
it was our sin that nailed HIM there, and this the world should know.
There is nothing we could ever do to deserve this love YOU give;
YOUR cross is our reminder that it's by YOUR death we live.
EMMANUEL our GOD with us who came to live inside
heart's that once were made of stone and filled with foolish pride.
Hearts that YOU have turned to flesh, who worship at YOUR throne;
because of YOU we are saved by grace and will never be alone.
YOU made us right before YOUR eyes so joyfully we praise;
we worship YOU the TRUTH, the LIFE, the ONE who is the WAY.
We gladly bear our cross and follow YOU, let YOUR will be our way;
no longer children of the night but children of the day.
The joy YOU give has been our strength, YOU'VE let YOUR voice
  be heard;
let YOUR love be our destiny, changing lives through YOUR
  unchanging WORD.

The Cross I Carry

I carry my cross upon me, in humbleness I yield
and cast away all of my pride, I'm not ashamed to kneel.
I've placed HIS WORD within my heart, its light has been my guide
this cross you see me carry, reminds me who's inside.
I knew life would not be easy, and no, it has not been
attacked from all directions, I still place my faith in HIM.
The one who shed HIS blood for me, who on HIS cross had died
whose body torn and beaten, who loved me more than life.
The ONE who on the third day rose to life, had won the victory.
Death where is your sting now? You have no place for me.
For when I'm persecuted for the ONE whom I believe
if I should sleep within my grave, HE will still return for me.
I'll be alive forever, HIS cross became my bridge
HIS blood was shed and by HIS death, yes, I'll forever live.
HE told me to take up my cross, to follow were HE leads
and said they persecuted HIM, and they will do the same to me.
HE also told me not to fear, but trust HIM and obey
that HE has overcome the world, and will return one day.
That HE will take HIS children home, when HIS trumpet will proclaim
"Come up, my beloved. All who've known my name."
"All who've lived their lives for me, who have trusted, who believed
who by faith received my grace, come and live with me."
That cross you carry on you, should not be one of shame
it should only make you humble to the ONE who called your name.

Be Still

Be still and listen to HIS still, quiet voice;
shut your ears from the loudness, the world's screaming noise.
Go to a place where GOD'S voice can be known;
HE will not be silent, you are not alone.
Be quiet and listen to all HE will say;
you will need our GOD'S wisdom throughout your day.
Do not say a word, don't shout or complain;
HE will give you an answer as you call out HIS name.
Be still as you listen and obey what HE'S said;
do not ask for answers if you will not move ahead.
Doing is better than saying a word;
because so many scream, they just want to be heard.
With so many voices that push and demand;
no wonder they are lost and do not understand.
Amidst all the confusion in these troubling times;
I need only ONE voice, and it sure isn't mine.
Be still in HIS calmness, HIS whispering voice;
block out the world and shut off its noise.
Turn off your TVs and your cellphones too;
HE wants you to hear HIM, but that's up to you.
Make the time to be still for HE has much to say;
if you need HIS guidance to survive the day, be still.
YOU did it all for us, because YOU loved us that YOU gave
that precious blood to cover us, our GOD, it's YOU who saves.

Just a Prayer Away

HE never sleeps nor slumbers, HE hears what you will say.
Are you tired and broken? HE is just a prayer away.
It was HIS SON who suffered, who died and rose again;
HE is our GOD ALMIGHTY, CREATOR, our AMEN.
HE hears when you are calling, and HIS will, will be done;
the answer to our prayers is found in CHRIST HIS SON.
Don't ever think HE'S faraway or that HE doesn't care;
just believe HE listens, HE hears your every prayer.

The One

HE gave HIS life for many but is followed by so few
it's not so much the words we speak, but more by what we do.
The ONE who bled and suffered, who loved us more than life
who wants us to be Born Again, that HE first had to die.
To us HE said, "Take up your cross. You will bear pain and tears
but do not fear I'VE overcame, I'LL hold you through the years."
"You will be hated for MY sake, your enemy is real;
take up your armor daily to him, don't bow or kneel"
"He's like a roaring lion; he kills, he lies, and steals."
"I will go ahead of you and guard you from behind;
a thousand may fall from left to right; but remember, you are mine."
Take up your cross and follow HIM wherever HE may lead;
HE was, HE is the ONLY ONE, and HE will always be.
On the right hand of the FATHER is the ONE who intercedes.
HE is the ONE who loves us, who chose to be the way;
HIS WORD a lamp unto our feet, our only hope and stay.
When our FATHER looks upon us, we are viewed under the blood;
when HE said that it was finished, HIS grace became enough.
The WAY to GOD is found in HIM for all eternity;
HE is the ONE who was, who is, who will forever be.

His Love

For GOD so loved the world, HE gave HIS SON for us to die
upon a hill HIS blood was shed, as HE was crucified.
Without the shedding of that blood, we could not be saved
it covered all our sin and guilt, our penalty was paid.
It took the LAMB of GOD to cleanse, to wash away the stain
to save us from the fire of hell, HE took our shame and pain.
HIS body torn, HE is the bread, and HIS love will sustain
the wine HIS blood shed for a love which will never go away.
Sometimes the things, those happenings, those things which make
    us blue
can make us feel we are alone, but that is far from true.
EMMANUEL our GOD with us is right here by our side
HE loved so much HIS blood was shed, and eventually HE died.
But, friend, it does not end that way for HE came back to life
HE understands our every pain, HE came to make things right.
You see no greater LOVE for us was ever shown to be
HE is the ONLY WAY there is, HIS love has set us free.
If you feel sad at times, I'm sure that they will come your way
just trust in HIM, obey HIS WORD, believing as you pray.
HE makes a way where none is found, call out to HIM right now
believe that HE so loved you too, for HIS love knows no bounds.
HE proved it on that cross that day, believe for HE is TRUTH
for while HE hung upon that cross, my friend, HE thought of you.
HE cannot lie, HE'S coming back to take us who believe
to a place so beautiful, where fear or tears can't be.
In the twinkle of an eye, we will all be changed
but it took that cross to prove HIS love—HE is the ONLY WAY.

Freedom Flight

On wings of white
I make my flight
On whispering winds
and stars which light
my way.
I feel the breeze
beneath my wings
and meet the light of day.
Freedom
what a mighty gift
which only GOD can give
CHRIST
the one who conquered
death
so that I could live.
Beyond
heaven's awesome sight
on angel wings
of gold I fly.

Be Careful Where You Walk

Be careful where you walk, my son; this world is dark with sin;
always look ahead of you, for yesterday has been.
Do not look back as Lot's wife did; you see it was her fault;
because she did not let the world go, she became a pillar of salt.
Always pray GOD makes a way on this journey of your life;
be kind and love your fellow man; son, thrive to do what's right.
Walk by faith and do HIS WORD; HE will direct your path;
stay faraway from evil men and things which just don't last.
Be a man of GOD, my son; don't ever quit or sway;
you know right now I'm proud of you, because you listen to what I say.
"I'm glad that you're my son," I said. But you are GOD'S son too;
point the world to JESUS, be kind in what you do.
"So be careful where you walk," I said. "And to your heart be true."
He said, "Daddy, you be careful because I follow after you."

Miracles Happen

Believe in the ONE who knows all that is,
hold on to HIS hand, you will always be His.
Never lose hope or give up on your dreams,
for miracles happen if we believe.
Belief is the reason that we have come this far,
faith is the way we can reach for the stars.
Prayer is the way we approach our GOD'S throne,
HIS love is our proof we are never alone.
Miracles happen when there seems no way,
HE will show you HIS love and it will be okay.
HE said just believe and trust that HE can,
HE loves you so much and has a great plan.
A hope and a future, you will see one day,
HE holds tomorrow and HE has made a WAY.
When HE parted the sea, they walk through on dry ground,
their fear was gone, when the enemy drowned.
When HE fed the thousands with the little that was,
everyone thought that it would not be enough.
The loaves and small fishes became a great feast
and no one went hungry, all tummies were pleased.
And what of the time HE turned water to wine
healing the sick, when HE opened blind eyes?
When HE walked on water and spoke to the sea?
Yes, miracles happen, if we would only believe.

We Are the Light

JESUS, the LIGHT of the world, came to save,
to free us from death and the grave.
HE hung on a cross on a hill for our love,
and shed HIS blood for our sin;
HE said by our faith that HIS grace was enough;
it was nothing we did (it's all HIM).
Once we are called to come out of the dark,
repented and broken we win;
we will find we are strong by the power of HIS might,
and can overcome the longing to sin.
We become light that illuminates truth,
as we speak the words which HE gave.
We become children and accepted by HIM,
and become free from death and the grave.
let us shine and through HIM, the LIGHT of the world,
as we point to that cross on that hill,
where on the third day HE arose from the grave,
and HIS SPIRIT remains with us still.
Love as HE loves and be that bright light,
as you share the good news of HIS love.
There are others out there who need your prayers,
and your little bright light is enough.
For lights show the way in the darkest of nights,
when we can't see that there's hope to the way,
point to the cross and the reason HE died,
and just watch all the lives that are saved.

Don't ever hide that glow from inside;
do not fear what others will say;
you're a child of the KING, for you chose to believe,
the LIGHT of the TRUTH and the WAY.

Call It What It Is and Keep Dancing in the Rain

Little daughter dancing, dancing full of glee
hopeful that the days ahead are all that they can be.
Call it what it is, my child, as joyful as you are
no doubt will ever change the fact, you are my shining star.
Call it what it is; it's love, the love of life and dreams
this faith you have just can't be hid, believing it will be.
So hold on to the hope you have, keep dancing in the rain
it shows that GOD'S not letting go, regardless if there's pain.
GOD is faithful and cannot lie; HE has great plans for you,
by faith in who HE is my child
HIS grace will see you through.
Call it what it is and praise HIM all your days
HE holds you close you're so much loved, keep dancing in the rain.

On the Wings of Your Prayer

HE gave me peace when I had only despair
HE gave me joy when it seemed no one cared.
HE lifted my life that was turned upside down
HE was by my side when no one else was around.
It started the moment when I first realized
I was lost and in darkness; I was broken inside.
I called out to JESUS, though HE first called me
I was chained to my sin but HIS blood set me free.
HE saved me from hell, an unquenchable fire
my heart became flesh and HIS love my desire.
HE finished HIS work on that cross on Skull Hill
HE came into my heart; HE is here with me still.
In this flesh I'm not perfect, but one day I'll be changed
in the blink of an eye, I will not be the same.
Never to ever suffer again
I will know only joy, a peace without end.
It's not only for me cause HE died for you too
call out HIS name, turn from sin as you do.
On this journey you take, you will need a best friend
HE will be all you need, the Beginning and End.
The beginning of life, HE is faithful and true
the reason HE died is because HE loved you.
HE'S that peace you have longed for in this life of despair
HE will never forsake you; HE will always be there.
Call out, HE is listening on the wings of your prayer.

Almost There

My tiny life begins; my heart has its own beat,
In Latin I'm called little one, with little hands and feet.
My tiny lips, nose, ears, and tongue can now be clearly seen
I'll be excited when I'm born, but excuse me if I sleep.
I'm now four months and I can taste, through Mommy I am fed
but I'm still too young to understand why Daddy wants me dead.
At four months old, I sleep a lot; you know sometimes I dream;
I'll grow up to make you proud; you'll love me I believe.
My hair is growing and I can smile, if you could see me now!
I'm almost five and still alive; I've come this far somehow.
My mommy now can feel me kick, my way to tell her how I feel!
My way to show that I'm alive and well, that I've always been for real.
Now six months I can sit up strong
Mama, you'd be proud of me; oh, how much I've grown
You see, I have lungs of my very own.
Now seven months, I look around, I can taste and touch, sometimes
    I hiccup too;
I hear your voice and I know that, Mommy, it is you.
I am eight months, almost there; please wait till I've arrived
Tell Daddy I'm his little boy and to please keep me alive.
My daddy didn't want me; he said he'd leave you if I came
I will never get to know him or ever have a name.
Somehow he convinced you that I could not be yours
I was someone you could have loved, that you would have treasured
    and adored.
I want you to know that I felt the pain
That pierced inside my little brain;
I'm living now with JESUS, but I will never hear your tender voice
    again.

Less of Me and More of YOU

Sometimes I don't like who I see in the mirror of my mind
and it sometimes makes me wonder, "GOD, am I still that blind?"
I know that JESUS died for me on that cruel and rugged cross,
but I still sin and feel condemned; sometimes I feel rather lost.
That old man of my past sometimes returns, like he does not want to die;
I try the best I know to do, to repent and then deny.
"Create in me a heart for YOU," I cry as I pray,
"Deliver me from me," I ask. "Let that old me fade away."
"Cast me not away from YOUR presence," I plead;
"And take not YOUR SPIRIT from me."
"Restore to me the joy I once knew; by YOUR great deliverance, set me free."
"Whatever YOUR will, whatever will be
give me more of YOU and less of me."
"I know that I often get in YOUR way, of the plans which YOU have for me;
but I also know that YOUR love is great;
and what YOU'VE started YOU will complete."
"That is the hope I hold on to, that YOUR grace is all that I need."
"FATHER, I ask that YOU hear this prayer; give me more of YOU and less of me."
"YOU know what's right; GOD, show me YOUR way,
so I can have joy at the end of the day."
"I want to be free to not do as I do,
give me less of me and so much more of YOU."

It's What We Say and What We Do

It's what we say the words we speak that lift or tears away.
Do our words build or just break down? Yes, it's all in what we say.
Do we speak love or just scream hate? There is power in our tongues.
Do we think about the words we speak, before all is said and done?
The tongue, although so very small, as a match becomes a flame;
it will extinguish and destroy everything in its way.
there are times we should not speak; when it's what we do, not say.
Like smile for those who need a smile and hugs along the way.
Sometimes it's what we do that counts much more than words can speak,
such as giving to the hungry and helping those in need.
Without words so much is done, like giving to a worthy cause,
when we freely give our hearts away without expecting applause.
When what we say and what we do encourages a life
what is done for them is done for GOD and that, my friend, is right.
So be that light to those who need, a light to guide their way
share that hope you hold on to, just give that love away.
Encourage each and everyone; we are family you will find;
so walk by faith, it is the way; leave no one behind.
If we speak love and walk that way, if how we live is true,
if by GOD'S grace we've chosen life, we've done what JESUS would do.
If what we say and what we do builds a life in need
than we have done what we must do, for each word and deed are seeds.
We are the sowers of the seeds of what we say and do
and will be judged by GOD one day, who is faithful and true.
HE will judge sin and when HE does, what will HE say then?
"Welcome home, my faithful one" or "You cannot enter in!"

Just Believe

Do not be afraid, just believe in the ONE
who gave us a gift wrapped within HIS own SON.
Who loved us so much HE was willing to die
as HE cried out in pain on a cross crucified.
But if you don't believe that HE did it for you
then you should fear HIM who is faithful and true.
For judgment is coming as a thief in the dark
be ready HE'S coming so don't miss the mark.
Sin has a way of distorting the truth
it's not what you say but more what you do.
Don't be afraid is said to the ones
who by grace and their faith believe in GOD'S SON.
And who such as fruit on a tree can be known
if they live for HIM or choose to be on their own.
Who walk in their pride and blink with the eye
they will not escape the ONE who they choose to deny.
Do not be afraid of what man can do
for man can't save the soul that GOD put within you.
"Fear not," is written in GOD'S WORD of TRUTH
HIS grace is sufficient; it is truly enough;
but if it's not studied or read, you can't know
the height or the depth or the width of HIS love.
Don't be afraid as HE molds you HIS way,
for HE is the POTTER and you are the clay.
HE is the AUTHOR of a story so grand
so don't be afraid, just take hold of HIS hand.
HIS WORD will not come back unaccomplished, my friend,
HE completes what HE starts and there will be an end.
An end to all teardrops, all the pain you've been through

when HE said, "It is finished!" HE did it for you.
HE rose from the dead, yes; that's the good news!
The ONE WAY to heaven who is faithful and true.
Just believe.

Let It Go

Bitterness bites; it has teeth made of blades
it spreads as a cancer of the thing it has made.
It has no place in a heart made for love
it destroys from within and it can't get enough.
An offense put upon us, an armor of nails
its heart is so black; it defiles as it wails.
It screams as it gathers all the hate which it breeds.
Guard your hearts and be humble as you get on your knees.
Do not allow it to have a place in your soul
give it to GOD, my friend; "Let it go."
Bitterness is a spirit; it festers as a wound,
if left unchecked, it will destroy family and
friends; all the love within you.
Bitterness is a seed but grows as a weed
a root of pure evil which none of us need.
Be holy as GOD is; be set apart
for this foul stench of bitterness has no place in our heart.
Do not be stubborn or think it's okay,
do not cheapen GOD'S grace; do not get in HIS way.
Repent of this sin for GOD'S mercy is great;
let the bitterness go before it's too late.
As a single match lit in a forest, it spreads as it wills,
it will bring upon death; it is love that it kills.
Let it go; it will drive you completely insane
it destroys everything that gets in its way.
The battles we fight in our minds can't be won
if we hold onto hate and not the love of GOD'S SON.

So let go of the things that will just hold you down
hold on to love, that's where joy can be found.
"Let it go."

What Should I Do?

What should I do, FATHER? YOU have the plan
I submit to YOUR will for my life's in YOUR hands.
Should I go straight? To the right or the left?
YOU give me hope; YOU decree every breath.
I would be lost without YOU; YOU'RE the hope that I need
I am YOUR child; YOU want the best life for me.
If I asked for bread, YOU would not give me a stone
YOU came into my heart and never left me alone.
What should I do, FATHER?
Let me do what is right
for YOU are my light
in the darkest of nights.
Once I was lost and my eyes were so blind
YOU found me and saved me said, "child, your mine."
YOUR love is the reason I have been made brand new
FATHER, give me direction in all that I do.
YOU gave me a heart made of flesh, not of stone
so that it may be known;
the TRUTH and the WAY and the LIFE that I need
YOUR SON shed HIS blood, yes HE did it for me.
I will go as YOU lead and do as YOU command
it's YOU who I need for my soul's in YOUR hands.

Tears in a Bottle

Our GOD keeps our tears in a bottle;
just to show us HE'S always been there,
in all of our griefs, all our sorrows;
as we weep in our pain, HE'S aware.
HE has held us though we could not see HIM;
at the time we were blind in our pain,
HE carried us all through the storms in our lives we will see,
for just one set of footprints remained.
GOD saves all our tears in a bottle;
all those good tears which we cried,
remember our tears are not wasted;
they bring HIM close to our side.
HE is close to the brokenhearted,
who are humble, who cry out HIS name.
When our spirits are crushed, there are reasons;
it is then we will find that HE saves.
It is when we become truly humbled,
when we see we can't make it alone;
it's through faith by HIS grace that we call out HIS name;
we will know that we are HIS own.
Our FATHER brings HIS children correction;
for HE loves us much more than we know;
sometimes correction is painful;
but it proves HE will not let us go.
HIS SON, in HIS love through obedience,
chose to die on that cross for our sin.
When you cry just remember HE loves you;
don't think of yourself, think of HIM.
Think of HIS pain when they nailed HIM to that cross,

the shame HE went through;
think of the blood which HE shed out of love,
as if HE did it only for you.
Think of the stripes on his back that HE took,
the flesh that was ripped clean away;
that spear that was thrust in HIS side as HE died,
for a debt that we could not pay.
Yes, HE keeps all our tears in a bottle;
don't forget that HE too also cried.
HE proved HIS love on that cross on that hill,
as HE was crucified.
HE died and was buried in a borrowed tomb,
then after three days rose again;
as he sits at the FATHER'S right hand,
HE prays for the ones He calls friends.
The tears we have shed all have reasons,
for each one has pointed to HIM;
we all have gone through these seasons of life;
but they are results of our sin.
GOD does not find pleasure if the wicked,
should die without receiving this gift HE'S bestowed;
JESUS wept for many who would die in their sin,
that number of HIS tears can't be told.
So each time you cry please remember;
HE has your tears in that bottle to show.
HIS love goes on without measure;
Don't think HE will ever let go.

He Called Me Out of Darkness

I was born in darkness and empty without truth
my life was utter chaos, afraid throughout my youth.
I walked without direction and stumbled in my ways
all I possessed was sorrow, in my bitterness afraid.
Dysfunction was a byword in the family where I grew
we did not know this JESUS, the WAY, the LIFE, and the TRUTH.
All that I knew HE hung there upon that cross of pain
and no one ever took HIM down for that's where HE remained.
We went to church on Christmas, on Easter hunted eggs
I did not know HE rose to life; we were not taught that way.
My youth was very painful without the love I craved
my innocence was taken, all I wanted was the grave.
In all my pain and sorrow and my need to escape
I found that drugs and alcohol would get me through the day.
My heart was dark and frozen as I shivered in the night
and did so many awful things that I knew weren't right.
But one day, GOD had spoken; HE called me by my name
a friend invited me to church; this place was not the same.
Not like the one I visited only once or twice a year.
No, this place was different for I sensed that GOD was there.
HE called me out of darkness; HE proved HE was the LIGHT
for HE changed a heart of stone so cold and made me come to life.
HE came down from that cross and was buried in a tomb
in three days was resurrected to save us all from doom.
Yes, HE called me out of darkness and each day I love HIM more
now I have a hope and a life worth living for.
My journey isn't perfect, although each day I grow
and as I pray and search HIS WORD, there's so much more to know.
HE gave me beauty from my ashes and HE tells me not to fear

HE said HE would not leave me; HIS promise I hold dear.
That old life is dead and gone; now I walk a life brand new
each day I'm given is a gift which only leads to TRUTH.
YOU called me out of darkness, LORD. I praise your name each day.
Thank you, FATHER, for your love that will never go away.

Good Tears

I now can smile because of tears
the pain, the fear, those broken years.
For GOD had purpose in HIS plan
My tears? Released. I took HIS hand.
My FATHER knew from the very start
that all my tears would seek HIS heart.

But God

In the garden when man first sinned, where nakedness was found;
GOD had a plan to save mankind; yes, even then HIS love knew no bounds.
My life was dark and bitter, friend; I knew not hope at all,
my sin was all I knew to do, but GOD knew before I'd call.
I wallowed in that filthy mire, in all my shame and grief
I did not know of holy fire, nor have faith to believe.
But GOD had a purpose, a plan to set me free
HE gave me faith, showed the WAY in whom I would believe.
The love I'd lost those many tears were meant to strengthen me,
all of those years, the grief and fears, those times were meant to be.
Good tears came by knowing HIM and trusting in HIS plan
HE is the author of my life; my future's in HIS hands.
Yes, life was not so nice back then, but GOD had made a WAY
HIS love for me is all I need, to only HIM I pray.
Upon that cross CHRIST died for me, but GOD made HIM the WAY
HE raised HIM back to life and now I love HIM every day.
Without HIM, we can't do anything; we cannot even breathe
but GOD changed everything, my friend, by loving you and me.

His Will Be Done

It's awesome how the tide can turn when blessings come our way
and how GOD can make our darkest night become our brightest day.
We thought those storms would never cease when our lives fell apart;
GOD shows HIS love and knows just how to heal our broken hearts.
I've traveled many tear-filled miles, along my journey's way
and every time I prayed to HIM, my darkness turned to day.
It was not so long ago I wallowed in my pain
when all I loved was taken and my teardrops fell like rain.
When each new blessing came my way, I counted every one
but I also realized that GOD'S love for me was not always joy and fun.
It is in these lessons in our lives that we see our Abba's hand
when our eyes are opened and we understand.
that along with sunshine must come rain; with joy, there will be tears
for on this scale of life we'll see GOD'S hand throughout the years.
Sometimes those things we ask of HIM are not so good, you see;
it's then I say, "YOUR will be done. YOU know what's best for me."
If we gave our children everything without a single care
that would be enabling and it would not be fair;
for how could that be love at all, if we didn't even care?
Good and bad will come our way, both sunshine and rain
so we must count our blessings in joy, also in pain.
For when we pray HIS will be done, let's trust HIS perfect plan,
do not forget HE is our WAY and our lives are in HIS hands.

It's Not Over

My scars tell a story, the life I have lead,
the pain of my tears as I laid on my bed.
The nightmares that came when all hope seemed but gone
those words which cut deep that went on and on.
I remember my mom's words the day that she said,
"I wish you were not born!" spun around in my head.
The scars of my youth, all those tears I had cried
depression so deep that I wanted to die.
How did I survive all the pain of my past?
It gives me such pleasure; I'm so glad that you asked.
All those scars taught me lessons that although very low,
I learned about love and it started to grow.
Even though I walked through the valley of the shadow of death
my GOD gave me hope as HE gave me new breath.
I learned of HIS SON who bore stripes just for me
who died on a cross so that I could be free.
Those nails that pierced through both HIS hands and HIS feet
all for my sin, HE would die on that tree.
HE rose from the dead, walked away from that tomb
and moved into my heart, not a moment too soon.
As I look at those scars of my past now I see
when HE suffered and died, HE did it for me.
Because HE overcame, I'm now never alone
for HE took that old house and made it HIS home.
It's because of my scars and my need to be loved
that I search for the TRUTH, found HIS grace was enough.
My story's been sad but I have no regrets
the AUTHOR'S not finished because it's not over yet.

Tears to Rain

They thought I'd die an early death and saw me rather weak
they were all proven to be wrong through my adversity.
A single seed had grown between the questions of their doubt
for everything that I'd been through is now my victory shout.
I held on to the faith I had, for my GOD had a plan
HE helped me grow to look beyond; my life is in HIS hands.
With all those tears which I had cried the journey of my pain
not one was ever wasted for HE turned them into rain.
That rain has only made me grow to be the man you see
the cracks of life from where I grew in my adversity.
Don't ever doubt even in pain when your eyes are filled with tears
but walk by faith, GOD'S made a way to hold you through the years.
It was HIS SON upon that cross who died and cried in pain.
It was HIS blood which covered me and took away my shame.
It was HIS love that I now see, oh how my life has changed
those many tears had made me grow, for HE turned them into rain.

God Knows

There's not a thing GOD does not know, nothing HE cannot see,
we can't hide a thing from HIM, who knows all that will be.
GOD knows the teardrops we will cry before we shed a tear;
HE knows that pain we keep inside, our every single fear.
GOD knows our hurt although we try, to hide behind a smile;
There's nothing friend that we can hide; let's not be in denial.
GOD knows whenever we forgive or hold a grudge within,
HE knew before that we would try to cover our own sin.
HE sees and HE knows everything; trust me when I say,
JESUS knew that HE would be the ONE, the ONLY WAY.
HE spoke HIS WORD and it was so; like that, it came to be;
the day, the night, water, and sky, HE created all we see.
GOD, my friend, knew everything, that we would fall to sin
that we would one day need the WAY to bring us back to HIM.
HE knew HIS SON would choose to bleed to die upon that cross;
HE knew it was the ONLY WAY that HE could save the lost.
HE conquered death and rose to life so that we might be free;
that through HIS grace we might by faith, be saved if we would believe.
HE knows all those HE'S called by name; who walk in spirit and in truth,
who follow HIM and bear their cross; who more than say, but do.
Time is ever fleeting as vapor in the wind
that day is fast approaching when HE will judge all sin.
Are we prepared to meet the ONE who knows us through and through?
Don't you not know HE knows all things? The deepest part of you.

Those things inside you try to hide, that sin you won't let go
will all one day be brought to light; you can't say you didn't know.
Repent of every single sin that holds you like a weight;
be free, my friend, and follow HIM, before it's just too late.

A New Year's Poem

A new year has come, the old year's gone, I still resolve to carry on.
To bear my cross, to be content, for GOD'S good grace is never spent.
It's still the same as years gone by, this power of the blood of CHRIST.
So as this new year comes our way, let us resolve to never stray.
To never stop or ever quit, to make the very best of it.

The Laws of Life

The laws of life are absolute, GOD'S undisputed proof,
they govern everything in life, all we say and all we do.
They can affect our very soul's; GOD forgave so we forgive
if we do not then HE will not; that's just the way it is.
Both natural and physical, we deal with every day,
electricity can kill us or can be used to light the way.
What goes up must come down; we reap what we have sown
we cannot plant a fig tree and expect an apple tree to grow.
We can't get past; these laws of life can change our very own.
In one form or another, we will find that they exist
we don't get good things out of life without putting good things in.
That's just the way it is.
The opposite is very true; the same goes with the bad
when we in life sow bad things, it is sure we'll get them back.
GOD knows what HE'S doing from beginning to the end
HIS laws are HIS perfection, which only HE can bend.
Like walking upon water, with a word HE calms the sea,
like touching eyes which never saw and causing them to see.
Those miracles which JESUS did, turning water into wine;
as Moses in the exodus, the dividing of the sea.
GOD calls things that never were, causing them to be.
Like the feeding of the thousands with the little that was there;
HE has proven HE is mighty for HE saved us by HIS grace
HIS only SON was crucified, in love HE took our place.
GOD is the ONE who makes these laws, the ones of which I speak
HE makes beauty from our ashes, gives us strength when we are weak.
Yet for lack of understanding, people perish as they will
HE would teach us all HIS laws if we would listened and be still.
I don't speak of the laws of man for they change all the time;

traditions lead to foolishness, which keep us bound and blind.
Making it impossible to follow man's decrees
the laws of GOD are different for they bring us to our knees.
Our GOD is never changing; HE remains the same
we must listen to HIS still, small voice and do what HE will say.
Remember that these laws exist, created for our sake.
GOD'S wisdom can't be fathomed, this love HE has for us;
we must follow HIS commands and only HIM and obey
HE longs to give us good things, but HE will judge sin one day.
for the ones HE has redeemed, JESUS became the WAY.
HE does not rejoice if we die without HIM, in our sin
HE is knocking on your door right now; will you let HIM in?
Respect these laws HE'S set in place, love HIM and choose life,
HE gave the world HIS only SON; for us, HE chose to die.
When in the garden sin was found and nakedness was there,
an animal had to die to make us all aware.
Without the shedding of HIS blood, our sin would have remained;
HE had to die to cover sin; it was the only way.
With this similitude I see and now can understand
to cover sin one had to die; the two go hand in hand.
For if the blood was never shed to cover guilt and shame
we could not be forgiven; sin's penalty would remain.
They were driven from the garden for they outright disobeyed
and did not ask forgiveness, all they did was cast the blame.
Adam blamed GOD for giving HIM Eve and she put the blame on the snake,
instead of confessing that they were wrong, they died from the choices they had made.
GOD'S laws were in place in the garden; they reaped from the sin they had sown
and us, just as they, we have chosen our ways, every choice
we make are our own.
GOD in HIS love
wants our fellowship, that we trust HIM and obey;

So let us respect HIM for HIS laws of life. Why? Because HE made
    them that way.
Who are we to tell HIM what to think or what to say?
Never forget we are creations,
HE'S the POTTER and we are the clay.

Soul Search

Where is the fear of GOD in man
who don't know TRUTH nor understand?
Who worship things this world gives,
who are still dead but think they live?
There is no fear of GOD; it's true
when we call HIM LORD but fail to do.
When we cleave onto our selfish ways
and care not about the end of days.
As it was in Noah's time
they partied on and lived life blind.
They honored man and feared not GOD
on slippery slopes, they choose to trod.
With trickling ears, they walked blind
they knew not GOD but "feel good" lies.
Pulpits decked with Christmas trees
with Santa Claus, we teach kids greed.
There is no fear, only regrets
upset for gifts they did not get.
Who fear not GOD mind earthly things
all those lies which Satan brings.
Oh GOD, forgive for many know
these pagan ways and won't let go.
Where is the fear of GOD, I say,
when men praise HIM but won't obey.
Who curse and hate their fellow man
is LOVE so hard to understand?
The very thing this world needs
is to repent, get on our knees
and pray our names not blotted out

to go with HIM when that trumpet shouts.
For with vengeance HE will then return
I pray by then that we will learn.
For GOD will judge all sin that day;
will we fear HIM and walk HIS WAY?
We call on HIM, say HE'S our friend
yet walk as if this life won't end.
Where is the reverence HE deserves?
Where is the honor to HIS name?
When we search our hearts, we'll find the blame.

The Humble Entry

Many expected HE'D come in as a conquering king,
on a white horse to vanquish HIS enemies
but that was not the way it would be.
HIS disciples shouted, "Praise to the KING!"
excited by the wonders of GOD they had seen.
But his entry was humble, on a donkey's colt HE had ridden
as the disciples shouted praise and laid their coats on the road.
This angered the religious leaders that day
so out of jealousy said, "Why do your disciples praise you that way?"
HE said in return that if they kept their peace,
the rocks would cry out and the praise would not cease.
When JESUS came near to the city HE wept,
HE opened HIS mouth and its doom prophesied.
The stones of the temple would be thrown to the ground,
that the enemy's forces would the city surround
for although they had witnessed the signs which HE did
they failed to know HIM, to them HE kept hid.
Very soon after this they would shout, "Crucify!"
this humble KING would be set up to die.
On a terrible cross HIS blood would be shed
for the sins of mankind HE would die in our stead.
HE gave up HIS glory when HE was born as a man
this baby in a manger, the mighty I AM.
Those lessons HE taught us of the way we should be
to love just as HE did, as HE washed their feet.
On that day of HIS entry, they expected something else
but they never expected that HE would give us HIMSELF.

Let It Break

It's not about a heart of stone but a heart that's made of flesh,
my journey took me places, where I found I was a mess.
So many things had happened, all those tears that my eyes cried;
I was empty and I tried to fill a void so deep inside.
On that journey made of tears, as I wondered to and fro;
I locked myself inside a cage that would not let me go.
I tried to fill that empty void with things the world gave,
but all the while it did not lead; it pushed me faraway.
The drugs, the lust, and all that pride; those things that maimed and killed;
would not complete the emptiness that only CHRIST could fill.
In brokenness upon my knees, I surrendered to HIS love,
I believed HE died for me; HIS grace was then enough.
I saw life in a different way, where love and joy abound
the new words I began to speak had turned my life around.
Instead of death, I'd spoken life; instead of hatred, love;
this heart that once was made of stone was changed by GOD above.
When JESUS died and rose to life, HE finished HIS FATHER'S will;
HE made this heart that had no peace, so peaceful and so still.
Let your heart break; it's okay, for when you do you'll find;
a life worth living for our LORD, than the death you left behind.
So let it break, HE'LL make it new; you will be born again,
when once you were HIS enemy, you'll then be made HIS friend.

The Stranger

I met a hungry stranger, homeless just like me,
we shared the little food I had, as we talked there on the street.
He told me his story of how his life had come to be;
as I listened quite intently, how he sounded just like me.
It's funny as I listened to this man I met that day
his voice revealed no sorrow; it was joy which he conveyed.
He spoke about his children and how he missed them so;
he said he always prayed for them and told me there was hope.
Though familiar, not a stranger to sorrow or to pain,
his love for others showed me that as he, I was the same.
We enjoyed helping others on this journey of our life;
to share the love played forward; what we knew to be right.
He thanked me for the food we shared as we parted ways;
I was happy that I met him and I smiled all that day.
I could not help to think about the journey he had shared
and how my heart had felt for him, that I wanted just to care.
We were not rich, but needy, though our hearts reflected faith,
I was glad to meet him, this friend who came my way.
We enjoyed each other's company, but just met that single time;
I can't forget his smiling face for it looked the same as mine.
I knew where this joy had come from; my heart opened to see,
I heard a still, small voice inside, who said, "What you did, you did
    for ME."

Everlasting Love

GOD'S love is everlasting; it will never go away,
that day HE came into your heart, HE came inside to stay.
For HE so loved the world and though, the world did not love HIM;
HE bled and died upon a cross to take away our sin.
HE is the mark we all have missed; yes, every single one;
that's why HE died and rose to life, the WAY, GOD'S only SON.
HIS love for us is deep and wide so much more than we could know,
that day HE came to live inside, HE promised to not let go.
We are the ones who pull away as if we do not care,
but through it all, HE does not change, for HE is always here.
This life on earth is quickly gone to live our lives at ease,
and if you do not know HIM now, please bow upon your knees.
Reject the world and all its cares which make us pull away,
we must repent of what we do; there is a judgment day.
There are two ways which we can live, in spirit or in flesh,
so trust HIS love, just walk in truth and HE will do the rest.
When HE died upon that cross on Skull Hill on that day,
it was HIS love that placed HIM there and it's never gone away.
HIS love is everlasting; HE has saved me, this I know;
we are all redeemable; HE values every soul.
Our love for HIM is done by deeds, good fruit upon the tree,
so, friend, believe the love HE'S shown, HIS grace for you and me.
HIS finished work upon that cross has proved to me HIS love,
for it is all we'll ever need, much more than just enough.

Thinking of You

So much has happened over time; our teardrops seemed to never cease,
but through it all, you are still mine; my mind and heart remain at peace.
I sit here thinking of your love for me and this love I have for you
this sea between us can't divide this love so pure and true.
When GOD allows us to be one, together man and wife
the world will see it's meant to be to last for all our life.
For even though you're faraway and I long for your sweet touch,
I know inside you feel the same and love me very much.
It stands to reason how we feel, the many tears we cried,
throughout the seasons of our pain, you never left my side.
I'm still here, I'll always be; our GOD will make a way,
to join us both as man and wife on our blessed wedding day.
I sit here in the evening breeze and think of you again,
the women whom I dearly love, my closest, truest friend.
You will be with me someday, my queen across the sea,
I know our GOD will make a way for a love that's meant to be.

What's in Your Treasure Chest?

What are the treasures that you hold? The things that rule your life?
Trinkets made of finest gold? Your job, husband, or wife?
Are they the plaques upon your wall? The trophies which you prize?
What are the things you covet, friend? Those treasures deep inside.
What's in this treasure chest of yours that you will not let go?
Will you give it all to GOD, my friend? The lover of your soul?
That time you say belongs to you? Those things you dare not share.
What about your cell phone and the secrets buried there?
If GOD would ever look inside, tell me, what will HE find?
A heart which once was cold and dark, but now is sweet and kind?
Will HE find HIS WORD inside a heart once made of hardened stone?
Did you come to realize HE would have died for you alone?
Where your heart is you'll see, my friend, your treasure will be found,
by grace through faith it can be changed and turn your life around.
We must repent, believing HIM, and do what HE will say
for only HE has made the WAY from darkness into day.
Is love inside for GOD and man, for every breathing soul?
Does TRUTH abide inside a heart once made of rust to gold?
A love in which you say and do and in doing you obey.
It proves what's there inside your heart, which only GOD can change.
We treasure oh so many things, but can we let them go?
On judgment day when all's revealed, what will your heart then show?
Do you accept the love of GOD and what JESUS did for you?
Are you willing to obey the WAY, the LIFE, the TRUTH?
Or will you reject HIS name? (Friend, it's up to you).
One day soon, HE will return to take HIS children home.
Will you be in that number then? Or forever be alone?
The choice is yours. to fill that chest those things your heart desires;
what's inside your treasure chest?

The GOD of TRUTH/or the father of liars?
There's nothing I can do for you except to make it clear,
in heaven, sin can't enter in and I pray I'll see you there.
So fill that chest with all that's good; have faith, accept HIS love;
by grace, you can be saved through faith, but you must obey and trust.

He Finishes What He Starts

Be confident of this, HE who has begun a good work in you
will complete it until the day of JESUS CHRIST. (Phil. 1:6)

HE lit a fire deep within, which burns so strong and clear
I heard HIS still voice calling me, that's when my heart drew near.
I heard the good news of HIS love upon that rugged cross
HE shed HIS precious blood for me for I was blind and lost.
HIS love I've found is more than I could ever understand;
HE did not scream at me or curse, just said to take HIS hand.
That HE would wipe away my tears and hold me through the storms
that HE would never leave me and HIS fire would keep me warm.
I love my GOD, my LORD, and KING because HE first loved me
it was HIM who called my name and caused me to be free.
This journey which I've walked through life may be different than yours
but we've all had our share of grief, for when it rains, it pours.
HIS WORD I've found to be the TRUTH and HIS love for us the same,
for HE suffered and HE died for us, that's why to earth HE came.
So with your heart, cry out HIS name, in brokenness believe
HIS promises are tried and true, from us HE will not leave.
HE'S coming soon to take us home
with HIM where we'll forever be,
with no more tears or suffering
we are children of the KING.
Note: HE who lit that fire in you is able.

The Meaning of Life

Now I lay me down to sleep, for very soon I'll be with thee.
I'm old and lived a life this long; you've kept me safe and made me strong.
YOU have prepared me for this day; my LORD, with you I've longed to stay.
I may be missed, though I may not; it does not really mean a lot,
for you're the one who died for me, to be with you, my LORD and KING.
(YOU mean more to me than anything).

The Seed

By faith I see beyond today
and know that GOD has made a way.
Things aren't as they appear to be
for faith is what our eyes can't see.
We cry when doubt gets in the way
and oh, those things our mouths can say!
Words have power to change life's flow
those things that doubt will not let go.
So many times we only cry
we do not think to wonder why.
We say, "I must not be loved by GOD."
I find that statement rather odd.
I know HE loves us; there's no doubt
of this I choose to shout out loud!
For HE so loved the world (that's us);
HE chose to die upon that cross.
Don't ever say HE does not care,
it was our sin that placed HIM there.
I promise HE will make a way
if by our faith we choose to pray.
Believing GOD is just the key,
unlocking all HE has for me.
That seed of faith can only grow
if we hold on and don't let go.
The past is gone; today is here
Tomorrow's a thing we shouldn't fear.
For when the storms in life appear,
know by that faith, he's always here.
It's HE, the ONE who died for you,

the ONLY WAY, our LIFE, and TRUTH.
The AUTHOR of our destiny
the ONE in who we should believe
all started by a single seed.
It can move mountains in our way,
it's believing what we say.
For if we doubt, we won't receive
that very thing we don't believe.
Peter walked on water then,
but when HE took his eyes off HIM,
began to sink into the sea,
for doubt had canceled his belief.
It was GOD'S love and outstretched hand, which saved him when he cried.
When we by faith call out HIS name, HE will not let us die.
Belief is such a simple thing, this seed which HE bestows.
Just keep your eyes upon the prize; HE will not let you go.

The Bridge

As I cross this bridge my GOD has made
I understand the price was paid
by HIS own blood; CHRIST made the way
to turn my darkness into day.
This bridge not made of mortar wood or stone
or anything which is my own;
no deed which I could ever do,
"LORD, I'm so unworthy. It's all YOU!"
YOU are the WAY to the other side;
that's why YOU came; that's why YOU died.
It was your blood which paid the price
that I could cross to the other side.
So as I cross this bridge to life,
HOLY SPIRIT, be my guide
I choose to live, to do what's right
to live by day and not by night.
A treasure whom I've come to find
this holy WORD of GOD is mine.
I cleave to YOU for YOU are LIFE
so to this flesh, I choose to die.
The mystery is CHRIST in me;
true joy for all eternity.
My hope for glory is not lost
for YOU alone have paid the cost.
Thank you, LORD; all glory be
all praise to YOU eternally.
For this bridge built by YOUR love
I know YOUR grace has been enough.
For I believe, by faith I see

YOU built a bridge which led to me.
YOUR love came first, now I love YOU
not what I did but what YOU do.
YOU said YOU would not go away
for in my heart YOU chose to stay;
I need YOU each and every day.
My LIFE, YOUR TRUTH, the ONLY WAY.

Beautiful Feet

JESUS said to make disciples to tell everyone you see;
salvation has been paid for on HIS cross for you and me.
HE came, sent by the FATHER to prove HIS FATHER'S love,
born a baby of a virgin, obedient to the cross.
HE suffered, whipped, and beaten, more than a man could bear,
they gambled for HIS clothing as if HE were not there.
They spit and called out curses, and mocked the WAY and TRUTH;
as JESUS looked upon them, HE prayed;
"FATHER, forgive them, for they know not what they do."
HIS last words, "It is finished," as HE bowed HIS head and died,
the man became the LAMB of GOD, for us was crucified.
Put into a borrowed tomb, someone else's grave,
but on the third day rose to life, it was the only way.
This is called the gospel; good news for all who hear,
for the ones who love HIM, to all who HE calls near.
How beautiful are the feet that go, who share with one and all;
who love those called unlovable, who answer as HE calls.
Believing in HIS grace through faith, repented of their ways.
How beautiful are the feet that claim that JESUS is the WAY!
HE said to make disciples and teach the TRUTH in love,
regardless of the obstacles, HIS grace would be enough.
Listen to HIM calling you; block out the world's noise;
search for HIM with all your heart, to hear HIS still small voice.
Listen to your calling, for the SHEPHERD knows HIS sheep;
HE will lead you home, my friends; it's your soul that HE will keep.
HE said HE would return for us, the ones who live by day;
how beautiful are the feet of them who walk as they proclaim.
The good news—yes, the gospel—that lifts up the ONE who saves;
JESUS our MESSIAH, the ONE, the ONLY WAY.

But on the Third Day

Hold on to faith and still believe, our GOD of LOVE will never leave,
HE lives in hearts who love HIM so; my friend, HE'S never letting go.
Hold on.
Hold on to hope, there will come a day, when we will see the TRUTH, the WAY;
the LIGHT of man, GOD'S only SON, who on a cross the victory won.
Hold on.
Hold on to LOVE and don't let go; HE'S worth the wait, just trust and know,
it took HIS blood upon a tree to save the lost who would believe.
Hold on.
Upon a hill, HE bore our cross in utter pain and agony;
HE finished what HE came to do, to die for sin, to set us free.
Hold on.
HIS FATHER had to turn away, HE was alone, HIS heart would break;
HE paid a debt HE did not owe;
that's why HE will not let you go.
Hold on.
Buried in a borrowed tomb, our SAVIOR lay inside that room,
But on the third day;
rose again, for death had surely lost its sting;
upon our LORD, the KING of KINGS, hold on to the joy that brings.
Hold on to HIS saving grace, my friend; believe it's not the end,
HE'S coming back to take us home, to a place we've yet not known.
Hold on.

Just Be

Be who you were called to be, a child of GOD who's been set free.
Be strong, be bold, don't be afraid, for on that cross your debt was paid.
Come boldly to the throne of GOD; be careful how you choose to trod.
Fear only HIM who called your name, the LIGHT of man, the ONLY WAY.
Be free to choose the life you live, for you can change in spite of sin;
HE made a way so you could win. Be born again because of HIM.
Just be the little light you are; you will shine brighter than a star.
Point the way to freedom's cross, and help to lead the broken, lost.
Be who you were made to be; redeeming grace has set you free.
Be gentle as a dove in flight, but be courageous, ready to fight;
for family, strangers, all your friends; but never sway or just pretend.
Be true to yourself and GOD above, who sent HIS SON all for your love;
who on a cruel and lonely cross, has paid the debt to save the lost.
Who lived and died and rose again; the LAMB of GOD who calls us friends.
Repent of all your worldly ways, forgiven for the debt HE paid.
Be bold, be brave, courageous too, and serve the ONE who thought of you.
HIS grace by faith will set us free, if we would only just believe HIS SON.

Daughter of Grace

Caught in the act and dragged through the streets;
her clothing ripped and no shoes on her feet
Tossed to the ground to see what would be said;
with murdering hearts, they would stone her to death.
The LORD bowed HIS head as HE wrote on the ground;
HE knew men's hearts as HE looked at the crowd.
The ten words HE spoke then, silenced all sound.
"Let he who is without sin cast the first stone."
Then one at a time, they all fell to the ground.
The crowd walked away; no condemnation was found.
To convict this woman, for all sin is the same, as they saw their own sin
No, not one dared to cast the first blame.
"Where are your accusers?" the LORD went on to say;
but none could be found for they each went their way.
With fear in her heart, at the feet of the LORD,
she received GODs grace, the true gift of HIS WORD
"Not one has condemned you and neither will I, but go sin no more,"
is what the LORD had replied.
Oh! Daughter of grace, you were saved by HIS love,
seen as redeemable, HIS blood was enough.
Stand up and receive as you walk in the LIGHT;
HE saved you from death; you've been given new life.
A hope and a future, forgiven, set free;
it is by GOD's grace that through faith you believed.
Once you had darkness, forgotten and lost.
But now there is hope, at the foot of the cross.

He Doesn't Live Here Anymore

My heart was once an open door, I let so much come in.
I was lost and without hope, so deep in all my sin.
I did not think to count the cost or what I let inside,
my eyes were blind, my heart was rust, that door was opened wide.
This door of life with death inside, this house was not a home;
I often cried myself to sleep, how I felt so alone.
One day there was a knock outside; how odd I thought it then,
that the person on the other side would wait to let HIM in.
I saw the eyes of purest love, a smile which gave me peace and love I
    never knew;
I let HIM in the door which closed, but opened up to TRUTH.
HE said, "I hung upon a cross and died, but after, rose again."
"Will you believe it was for you, to take away your sin?"
That darkened house then filled with light, I said to HIM, "I do."
HE came to live with me that day, the WAY, the LIFE, the TRUTH.
But then one night I heard noise outside, someone trying to break in;
JESUS opened up the door saying, "I'VE taken all his sin."
"That person you are searching for does not live here anymore."
"He's born again and made brand new." HE then gently closed the
    door.
By grace through faith I then was saved; secure, my life had changed;
no longer lonely and ashamed; my house was rearranged.
I was a different person then, that day I let HIM in;
no longer taken by surprise and free from all my sin.
As I recall the words HE said, "HE doesn't live here anymore,"
I cried a tear of purest joy which I never knew before.
For on that very day I died, no longer wretched and poor;
the day my SAVIOR came inside and gently closed the door.
And so my friend HE freed me then, my house was made brand new,

I now can choose who comes inside, also the things I do.
The man I was no longer lives where death and sin abode;
where once my heart was made of rust, HE'S turned it into gold.

The Walk of Faith

I walk alone at times to think, but all the while my GOD'S with me
and even though I cannot see, I know HE'S here; I just believe.
All the promises HIS WORD conveys, I know HE is the ONLY WAY,
HE is my hope throughout the day, by faith I know I'll be okay.
See, I believe what I can't see; it's faith that goes ahead of me;
substance and evidence are things I see, knowing that my GOD'S
    with me.
And even though it's not here now; it's waiting there, I know somehow.
Our FATHER'S pleased with faith and truth, not what we say but
    what we do.
Faith is not just what we say; it's based on what we do;
so as HE opens up the way, it's up to us to follow through
believing that HIS WORD is TRUTH.
So with that said, believe and do.
It's not by works that we are saved, but works do prove our lives have
    changed.
GOD says we must be born anew; it's seen in what we say and do.
Without faith, we cannot please, for we must live in TRUTH;
believing that HE is the WAY to lead us to the LIGHT of day
for what HE says HE'LL do.
Our journeys end, we cannot see, but the AUTHOR knows what it
    will be.
Have faith and love your fellow man and love our GOD who holds
    your hand.
Have faith and walk the walk of light; do good for we know what's
    right.
Hope when it seems hope is gone, dance in the rain and carry on.
Faith is a gift our GOD bestows; hold on for HE'S not letting go.

Be Warned

GOD is stronger in our weakness; HE can save a humble heart
HE will lift you if you let HIM; for grace HE did impart.
But for those whose hearts are stony, who wink with eyes of pride
all who hate their neighbors and who push GOD's truth aside;
in love, I give you warning, if this is you I have described
reverence GOD and listen, toss away your foolish pride.
Although GOD loves you in darkness, HE must still judge sin;
if your name is not in the Book of Life, it's sure you won't get in.
JESUS shed HIS blood for you, for all the world HE died
on the third day rose again; HE is the LORD of life.
HE longs to do the same for you, to make you born again
but until you humbly call HIS name, you will die in your sin.

Rain Dancer

I started the day again with a frown;
my smile turned upside down.
The clouds appeared filled to the brim with rain;
they seemed to follow me dark and disdained.
My thoughts were mingled yet scattered abroad,
as I had a conversation with GOD.
"FATHER? Why am I still saddened by this pain of my past;
why can't these memories leave? My soul's so downcast!"
"All I can think of as I wallow in tears,
is this loss in my life, all the pain and the fears."
My GOD spoke gently, calming my heart.
"Son? Have I left you? I've been here from the start."
HE said, "Son, how I love you. Not once did I leave;
I was with you in sorrow and I hurt as you grieved."
"I've collected your tears in a bottle to show;
I was with you then and I won't let you go."
"Realize, my son, it's okay to let go of tears;
hold on to my hand as we travel the years."
"It may not appear I was there, like today in your gloom;
but I held you in love as you wept in your room."
"I understand loss; I'm familiar with pain;
but it's okay to dance in the rain."
"It's okay to express joy, even in pain."
I smiled as I listened to the words that HE said,
as I realize HE was with me when I found my wife dead.
HE gave me much comfort in my sorrow and pain;
so along with this smile now, I'll dance in the rain.
I must always remember that my FATHER is here,
that HE guides the way out of gloom and despair,

that HE will send others who walk the right way,
who will hug me and tell me that it will be okay.
I should never forget as I start each new day,
to give praise to my FATHER as HE guides my way.
That I can make choices and no matter how dark,
my candle stays lit as it illuminates my heart.
So if the clouds seem to trigger to cause my heart pain,
I can choose to be different and dance in the rain.

Who I Am

I am a young brave of the first nation,
proud and strong with memories of a time past.
I am a ring of fire on a cool, star-filled night,
listening eagerly as stories of my heritage are told.
I am a warrior of the plains on my painted pony, chasing the wind.
A hunter with bow and arrow who leaves nothing to waste.
Fed by the buffalo who do not know the closeness of their extinction.
I am a rattlesnake hiding near a cool rock,
while the scorching desert sun rests upon the land,
giving a warning for all who would dare approach and unafraid to strike.
I am a coyote howling at the moon, speaking to my brothers in the wind.
A majestic eagle who soars high above the clouds, able to see forever.
I am only one member of many tribes, all survivors.
Taught the old ways, yet living on a new frontier.
I am proud of who I am and will no longer be robbed of my dignity.
A son of a chief of the first nation, stolen from under our feet.
I am the sun which rises from the east,
hot and relentless, only being what my MAKER has said.
I am the night wind blowing, telling a story which has no end,
of a people stronger and braver than ever before;
whose regal past is only a reflection of a brighter future.
A people with true hearts which will beat forever.
I am who I am, and no man can ever take that away from me,
for my story will always be told.
I am the warmth of a fire which will not die;
my heart is free, and red is the only color I bleed.
My heart beats to the drum and the dance;
I am in rhythm with the earth and loved by my CREATOR.

Redemption's Story

I'm nothing, LORD, without YOU; YOU have the words of life;
I need YOU every single day to help me walk in light.
I had no value in my life; each choice I've made was wrong;
they had put me in dark places, where I did not belong.
For YOU, see, I was broken and in need of saving grace;
YOU took the stripes which I deserved; GOD, YOU stood in my place.
I am nothing without JESUS, my LORD, my PRINCE OF PEACE;
just knowing that you loved me first has brought me to my knees.
Just knowing I'm redeemable with value in HIS eyes;
that HE left the ninety-nine for me has made me realize,
that our FATHER wants relationship 'cause we are the family tree;
family, I need you the same, just as much as you need me.
HIS love for us is why HE died and HE gets all the glory;
the great news is that we are HIS; that is redemption's story.

His Will

We always pray, "HIS will be done";
and trust the blood of HIS own SON.
We say by HIS stripes we are healed
and know HIS sacrifice was real.
We did not see nor did we hear
yet still believe HIS cross of tears.
HE cried, "FATHER, why hath THOU forsaken me?"
HE bore our sins which set us free.
Yes, may our FATHER'S will be done;
for when we bend, we will not break,
we must believe the grace HE gave,
cry to HIM, call out HIS name.
HE said, "It's finished," as HE died
but on the third day rose again;
HIS love for us meant more than life
HE is the gift for every man,
for every woman, girl, and boy
HE is the source of purest joy.
HE bore the cross which should be ours
HIS hands and feet so deep with scars
but death could not keep HIM away.
HE said HE would return one day.
So when we say, "GOD'S will be done,"
remember JESUS, HIS only SON
The WAY to HIM, THE ONLY ONE.
Remember we were given life
HE chose to die to make things right.
We each have a journey which we must take;
sometimes it seems we get no breaks.

For storms will come along with rain
and through them we will feel the pain.
But with each drop, the roses grow
HE saves each one, this you should know.
Each and every tear we cry
one day, HE will dry our eyes.
Tears like rain are both the same;
don't forget from them come growth;
flowers bloom and lives do change
and from them both, GOD'S love you'll know.
For beauty from our ashes bloom
and hearts will change (believe this true).
For I've seen hearts as cold as stone;
along with this one I call my own;
What GOD can do with hearts of flesh,
who do believe HIS WORD is TRUTH,
who willingly will say and do.
Whose fruit is seen which praises GOD,
this pure LOVE the world finds odd.
You cannot hide the joy you'll know
if you but let this world go.
The fear of man will go away
and love for them will take its place.
Yes, pray in spirit and in truth,
for on that cross HE thought of you.
May our FATHER'S will be done
when we believe in CHRIST, HIS SON.

It's Not About the Storm

Don't take your eyes off JESUS, for storms will come your way,
and you can walk on water as Peter did that day.
The LORD told him to come and so he took a step of faith,
it's not about the storms we face, but in the ONE who is the ONLY WAY.
Keep your eyes upon JESUS, friend, for HE will calm life's storms,
HE will lead you in the way to a place secure and warm.
Tears will come to everyone; sometimes life seems unfair;
like you are left abandoned, as if nobody cared.
Life is like a testing ground to see how we will chose;
Do we believe and walk in faith? Do we walk within HIS truth.
Or do we doubt as Peter did, as he sunk into the sea,
he took his faith off JESUS and believed what he could see.
HE saw the waves the tempest blew, the fierceness of the sea,
and took his eyes off JESUS, the ONE he first believed.
But do not forget that as he sunk in his moment of despair,
he cried out for salvation for he knew CHRIST was there.
The love of GOD reached out to HIM and save him from his plight,
for compassion always can be seen when you look into GOD'S eyes.
GOD'S hand reached out to save him and HE will do the same for you.
HE said HE would not leave you; HIS promises are true.
So when the storms in life do come, remember HE is there;
keep your eyes upon HIM; HE is as close as your next prayer.

He Loves You

HE loves you with a love so grand that HE chose to die for you,
I know it's hard to understand but your heart knows this is true.
We were not there upon that hill when that spear had pierced HIS side;
HE took our sins upon HIMSELF so we would be made right.
Because of HIM, Adam's curse was lifted from our lives.
HE rose again, the scriptures say, and that should be good news;
HE'S the way to heaven; on that cross, GOD bled and thought of you.
HE loves you with a love so true and sealed HIS bond with blood.
By faith you chose to walk THE WAY, where HIS grace would be enough.
HIS love for you is wonderful, so much more than words can say.
HE is LOVE, the Son of GOD, the ONE, the ONLY WAY.

A Glimpse of the Past

This crystal pond of memories, oh, how the days have flown;
I never thought this day would come when I felt so alone.
Those yesterdays have gone away, and with them all who died;
the pain is so familiar, for I know that we all cry.
Sometimes the times sneak up on us; we sit with awe, amazed,
and wonder just what happened to the joy along the way.
We are as a mist, my friends, a vapor in the wind,
in need of GOD'S salvation to take away our sin.
Of all I've learned these sixty years, as I look into this pond,
we must love GOD and love your fellow man before our time has gone.
Smile with those who need a smile and give your heart away;
cry with those who weep, my friends, for you'll need that one day.
Repent of all those early ways and trust in our FATHER'S plan.
Believe in HIM who loves you so, who wants to take your hand.
Respect your parents here on earth; you're only born with two.
Search for understanding and always love what's true.
For time flies ever quickly and before you know it's gone;
then all we are, are memories, a reflection in a pond.

Out of Darkness

Let there be light, HE said;
and it was the will of the only I AM;
creation was spoken but first came the light;
Alpha of all who GOD is, all given by HIS command.
The SPIRIT of HIM hovered the deep,
and every unreachable part of the heavens above.
Man was created by HIS breath,
and he woke receiving the proof of HIS love.
The light of the world had then shone on man,
to direct us so that we then might see,
the hope of the world in HIS time would shed blood,
to save a sinner like me.
Born of a virgin, the WORD was made flesh,
the one SON of GOD born to die;
the grace HE has given, the love which HE is.
Come out of darkness and run to the FATHER of light.

Peace through Grace

It is by grace that peace abounds,
I so delight in this joy I've found.
By HIS shed blood I've come to know
a love who won't let go.
Though times are hard and the storms may come
when we feel like we are alone.
Hold the hand of the SON of GOD;
on who we wait to take us home.
Peace is found by HIS grace alone, the shed blood on the cross;
to reconcile us to HIM who found us; though we were lost.
Hold on to the ONLY WAY to our FATHER'S heart above;
who sent HIS only SON to us, the full expression of HIS love.

Since You've Been Gone

It's been a while, since you've been gone;
I miss you, oh, so much.
The way you always smiled at me;
the warmth of your gentle touch.
It seems you're always on my mind, especially when I'm blue;
though I can say on sunny days, I often think of you.
Since you've been gone, I've carried on, to face the coming day;
it's true I wished you were not gone, that you never went away.
Since you've been gone so much has changed; the world seems dim
    and dark;
But, Becky, when I think of you; it brightens up my heart.
It was so hard to let you go, the many tears I cried;
if you could hear me now I'd say, "I often wondered why."
I've learned it was your time to go; GOD needed you with HIM,
I've also faced reality that every life must end.
Since you've been gone, I've found someone, who loves me more
    than life,
and one day soon, I'll marry her, and she will be my wife.
I know you'd love her as a friend and sister in our faith;
her name is Beverly, my heart; she's proof that JESUS saves.
I turned to stone the day you left; Oh, how my heart froze;
I didn't really want to live, my love; the sadness only grows.
This new love, my Beverly, my queen across the sea;
she helped me realize that I could live, though you were not with me.
I know she loves me very much. Did you send her here to me?
She's become my angel; her love has set me free.
You said you didn't want me to be alone, to mourn until I died;
I did not realize how fast it was, the day she came inside.
She said she fell in love with me; she said because of my heart;

and since that night that I proposed, our love's not been apart.
She lives across the deep blue sea; but it's as if she were right here with me;
I have no doubt she'll be my bride, for this was meant to be.
Becky, I know that we will meet on the day I'm heaven bound;
I know you're pleased that I can rejoice, in the new love I have found.

A man who finds a wife finds a good thing. (Prov. 18:22)

My Love for You

This love for you, my darling, reaches far beyond the blue;
so much deeper than the ocean is the love I have for you.
My love for you is higher than a bird can fly,
beyond the tallest mountaintop, much wider than the sky.
Time will not erase this nor can vision take from view,
this special place within my heart reserved for only you.
You are in my every thought, where day and night do meet;
you are the dreams I dream; that's who you are to me.
Beverly, my future bride, the only one I need.
As I walk among these roses, while I smell the fragrant air;
the awesome beauty of these flowers next to you cannot compare.
More refreshing than cool water from the desert's scorching sun;
you're the woman I desire; yes, you are the only one.
Knowing that you love me back makes my heart skip a beat;
you are the air which keeps me breathing; that's what you are to me.
No, nothing can compare nor can ever be so true
than the knowing of my heart, this love I have for you.

The Power of the Tongue

LORD, forgive me for those things I've said, not pleasing to your ear.
All those doubts, that from my mouth, brought unbelief and fear.
Those cutting words which hurt the ones, which I love very dear;
can push away the very ones, which I need very near.
Forgive me for the times that I spoke death instead of life;
which caused bad things, those happenings, that somehow ruined lives.
Please set a guard upon my lips so that I just speak life.
Remind me, LORD, that when I speak, I can cause a soul to die.
This tongue can be an evil thing, when used improperly;
it only shows what's in my heart, those lies which I believe.
LORD, better yet, I ask of you, please take this heart of stone;
and let it be a heart of flesh, that will touch your very own.

Under Bridges

Under a bridge, they gather, for it's nearly time to feed,
for with these homeless of this city, there always is a need.
Young and old they meet here, and with food and clothes are blessed,
not all are addicted; they just landed in this mess.
Through many circumstances and moments of distress;
some well-groomed, some dirty, they all came here to be blessed.
These homeless of these cities, it all seems quite the same,
some wallow in self-pity; some never cast a blame.
The stories are all different of how this came to be,
as some are wise and humbled, while some refuse to bow the knee.
Some were robbed of everything, all which they possessed,
while others only choose to take, causing much distress.
Slowly, they all gather as gospel music plays;
so many will just choose to take while few of them are saved.
Tomorrow, it will be the same underneath this bridge,
again as many take advantage and few will say amen.
Thanking GOD for the blessings that are soon to come their way.
It will be the same tomorrow, for most just another day.
Throughout the many cities, as servants hear the call
to truly love their neighbors as they give their all.
What is done for the least of these is done unto our GOD
where love is unconstitutional, this world sees as odd.
The LORD, HE gives and HE takes away; HE builds and HE tears down;
when pride will dare to take a stand, it's tossed upon the ground.
HE will not despise a humble heart repented of its ways;
so call out to HIM for mercy; this is your salvation day.
You may not always be here friends, lives do change.
It all depends on choices and where our feet do trod,
follow HIM, HE loves you, and touch the hand of GOD.

Hold On to the Joy

I'm not the same, I've been transformed
that old me doesn't live here anymore.
So much has changed, it's not the same
when joy came knocking at my door.
That old me died so long ago
I really don't miss the way (he) was
and so I must forget.
Because I'm not the same.
This journey which we take called life
full of struggles, hard to bear.
lessons from the school of hope
I give GOD all my cares.
I've been transformed by GOD'S good grace
that's why I smile.
O the joy these good tears cry
because of hope that grows inside.
Forgive, forget, the past is that.
Hold on to the joys in life.

I Am Found

I was that sheep who lost my way;
perhaps it's the reason that I strayed;
for it was my way which made me lost;
I did not think to count the cost.
I chose what pleased me; this I found;
my ways were wrong; they were not sound.
They only took me faraway;
that darkness caused my heart to stray.
Only GOD could find me then;
HE left the ninety-nine (amen).
The SHEPHERD of my soul found me;
the ninety-nine were safe, you see.
I was that silver coin, gone lost;
but it was when HE found me gone.
HE searched wherever I could be;
and in all that searching, HE found me.
For I had value in HIS eyes;
My worth is what had made HIM cry;
HE loved me more than I could know;
that's why HE never let me go.
HE could have said, "I still have nine";
walked away, left me behind.
My GOD had found me then rejoiced;
I'm grateful that I heard HIS voice.
I was the son, who went my way;
to live my life in sin that day.
To foreign lands; 'twas I who strayed.
I wanted things not good for me;
and left my FATHER'S love, you see.

I spent everything I had;
thought it was good, but it turned out bad.
I wallowed in the filth, that mire;
and missed the love of holy fire.
One day as I in the gutter lay;
I had a change of heart, I'd say.
I wanted the joy I had back then;
confessed in how I chose to sin.
While I was still a great way off,
my FATHER ran, for I was lost.
HE ran and hugged me back to life;
and freed me from my guilt and strife.
I was lost, then I was found;
I found that grace and love abound.
That FATHER will not let me go;
but I had to repent, so I might know.
That though I once was lost, you see,
It was my FATHER'S love for me;
that brought me back from death to life;
from being wrong, then knowing right.
If you feel that you've gone too far;
it does not matter who you are;
call out to HIM; HE hears your voice;
at that point, know you have a choice;
to remain lost or heaven bound;
I made my choice because I'm found.

Luke 15:3–32

Praise

I praise GOD for the little things that bless me every day;
the smile of a stranger who I pass along the way.
For flowers and for butterflies, all the beauty that I see;
I praise GOD for the saplings which grow into mighty trees.
We take for granted many things along our journey's way,
stop to smell the roses and praise HIM for each day,
for every time HE wakes us up, for every breath we take.
I praise HIM for the little things, a ladybug in flight.
For every star that I can see on a moonlit night.
Everything created are gifts our GOD bestows,
I praise HIM for my mustard seed of faith which only grows.
I praise GOD for the small and large, all that my eyes can view;
but most of all, O family of GOD, I praise HIM for each of you.

Our Dream

Speak to me softly, O bride of my dream.
Tell me you love me from over the sea.
As we pray together, your heart's here with me.
I'll speak to you softly as I understand
and promise to love you to be a strong man.
To hold you, protect you, safe under my wing,
to whisper, "I love you," my sweet Beverly.
My lady of wonder, I love you as myself,
no one can replace you; there is nobody else.
You've held my heart gently and have prayed though the years,
our moments together, in spite of our tears.
Without you, my life would not mean much to me,
this love that we treasured is a love meant to be.
Mahal kita, my beauty, my bride across the sea;
praying that soon, you will be next to me.
I thank you for loving me back all this time,
I pray that you'll always decide to be mine.
I pray that GOD'S angels would bring you to me;
to be us and our children in complete unity.
Our sons and our daughter from the faith of our love,
a gift by our MAKER from heaven above.
When we are united, when we kiss and hold hands.
You will know by my eyes that I'm truly your man.
We will walk hand in hand on the shore of our dream.
Together in love, as it is meant to be.
This hope just grows stronger as we build this new life.
I'll soon come to get you, my children and wife.

As I Wait

As I was upon the LORD for the next step I must take;
I trust HIM that HE knows what's best, that HE guides me for my sake.
That my GOD has a plan for me, much better than my own;
that I must wait for HIM to lead me, as the next step I am shown.
My GOD is everywhere there is, and nothing from HIM is hidden;
HE knows our ways and all we are, all we ever said or did.
HE knows all that we will say and all that we will do;
every intention of our hearts, to HIM, is in plain view.
With that, I trust HIM and believe that HE will surely lead;
that HE will take me to a place that covers all my needs.
That my strength will be renewed and my faith will grow;
My life is in my FATHER'S hands for everything HE knows.
In this world, it's hard to wait on things, for fears get in our way;
we don't know what tomorrow brings or if we will survive today.
One thing we must realize and I pray we understand;
that everything—yes, everything—is in our FATHER'S hands.
When JESUS taught us how to pray, our FATHER'S will is best;
by faith, we then must trust in HIM, as we wait and rest.

Worship

Worship to me is giving, giving all glory to GOD;
It's taking all that I'm created to be, and giving it back with my heart.
Worship is praise to the one SON of GOD, HIS dying as HE took my place;
it's pouring my life back out to HIM as I honor and cry out HIS name.
Worship changes the atmosphere and I never am just quite the same.
Worship is a song, a dance, or a rhyme; it is art to the MAKER of all;
worship is giving ourselves of our time, our expression as we answer HIS call.
It is loving GOD first with the fruit which we bear, and in loving each other as one;
it is so much more than mere words can express;
it's the love which we do as we honor and worship GOD'S SON.

Love

What is love?
Is it just a word?
No.
It is something done,
and not just heard.
The Bible says that
GOD is love;
HE proved it at the cross;
HE gave the very best
HE had
so that HE could
save the lost.
It took the blood of HIS
own SON;
Who died so horribly,
JESUS chose to die
that way
to redeem both you and me
(love does).
It will move mountains.
It sets the captives free.
Love gives so much more
than only words.
It loves.
Unconditionally.
Long before we were
ever born;
GOD loved us as HIS own.
HE loved us long before

HIS love for us
was ever known.
Love is not just
a thing we say;
it is a thing we do.
It hugs and holds;
it gives away.
A love that does
is true.
We needed an example
of what this love could be;
but it took the willing
heart of GOD;
And HIS blood upon
that tree.
That cross is a reminder
of how our love should be.
In order to accept HIS love;
we must, by faith, believe.
I believe that JESUS is
the ONLY WAY;
to save one such as me.

God is Enough for Me

GOD is enough; I have all I need;
the blessed assurance that HE'S always with me.
HE leads me by waters, so wonderfully calm;
HE is my SHEPHERD who will do me no harm.
HE will always sustain me; that is why I'm content,
to follow HIS leading to wherever I'm sent.
The LORD is my SHEPHERD and I am HIS lamb;
HE will protect me, wherever I am.
The stripes on HIS back and the blood that HE shed;
HE did it for love, for HE died in my stead.
All I could want or ever will need, comes from HIS hand;
I have a hope and a future for it's part of HIS plan.
HE rose from the dead, three days after HE died;
so that I could forever be right by HIS side.
Yes, GOD is enough, friend; trust HIM, you'll see;
it's all done by grace and a heart that believes.

The Lighthouse in the Storm

When days were calm and times were bright;
we smiled with joy at the sight;
for we could see that things were fair;
the summer breeze and fragrant air.
The family ties were held on tight
and love was there, when things were right.
We laughed and sang without a care;
for we were with our loved ones there.
But as time passed, our smiles would fade;
when we saw death and times were gray;
we watched our loved ones fade away.
We saw that good times come and go;
they hit us hard; how could we know?
That things could change so rapidly;
that tears would bring us to our knees?
The storms of life were dark and gray;
the rain hit hard as lives would sway;
and many went their chosen way.
Some thought that drugs would ease their pain
or alcohol would numb the brain;
and many would not be sane again.
They lost all hope for better days.
Too bad they did not look for light;
to guide them through those storms in life;
to navigate them through the night.
To reassure them, storms do fade;
that faith would show them all the way;
and GOD would lead them to the day.

When ships are caught in stormy gale;
when frantic wind would rip the sail;
the sailor looked into the dark of night
for the lighthouse and its guiding light;
a light to save them from the storm;
to a place, secure and warm.
In the book of John, I read one day;
how GOD came to earth to guide our way.
How HE was born the LIGHT of man;
and how we then did not understand.
HE came as a child, and yet divine;
the very ONE who made all things;
the LIGHT of LIFE; would we believe?
The ONE who guides our destiny.
CHRIST, the savior of mankind;
had a plan that HE should die;
to save us from our sin inside;
to make us clean and give us life.
Just believe in HIM, not man;
and HE will make you born again.
The storms in life will come and go;
I've been through many; this I know;
that I can trust my LORD in them;
HE is the light to every man;
to every woman, girl, and boy;
the ONLY ONE who can give joy;
for in the morning joy will come;
when we've learned to trust GOD'S only SON.
The lighthouse in the storms do save;
if in life's darkness, we are lost;
it shows the way we need to go;
reminds us JESUS paid the cost;
with HIS own blood to save the lost;
HE is the only way I know.
HIS love has always calmed my storms;

HE'S kept me safe, secure, and warm.
For GOD so loved the world; that's us;
in HIM we should believe and trust.

One Foot in Front of the Other

I just want to encourage you as you walk this path with GOD,
do not forget HE never leaves; remember with whom you trod.
At times, the path seems crooked, friend; like you walk this way and that;
it still remains the path your on, no matter where you're at.
There will be times you feel alone, as if there were no brothers;
just move ahead and walk the path, one foot in front of the other.
Never quit in spite of storms, when things get in the way;
have the faith that the path you're on will lead you to the WAY.
Place one foot in front of the other, friend, for with each step you grow.
GOD'S grace and faith will lead you to the place you need to go.
It is a race we all will win, but it matters not our speed,
our faith will grow if we don't quit;
it will just increase.
HE will be back to take us home, my sisters and my brothers;
but only when we walk the path, and place one foot in front of the other.
for only then we will see the end as we look upon HIS face;
remember that the way we walk is a walk and not so much a race.

What I Know

I understand you don't know me, but you have read my rhymes.
I've been here to encourage you, to get you through hard times.
What I know is what I hear from comments that you share;
I give all the glory to GOD for always being here.
I understand they made you think, these words that I convey,
I praise the LORD your hearts were touched in a special kind of way.
My story is a mystery that some of you don't know;
but understand my life been hard though I'm not letting go.
For three years now since my wife passed, the many tears I've cried;
I could have quit so long ago and given up on life.
Thank GOD for homeless shelters for a place to rest my head;
but it's not the same as your own home in your comfy little bed.
Don't get me wrong but what I've learned that my *yes* is always *yes*.
What I know, I've lived through it and I live there still.
My word to me means everything, if I can do it then I will.
The streets have taught me many things, as I struggle through it all;
to not give up in the hope I have; and to get up when I fall.
I know my GOD takes care of me; HE has proved it time and again;
I can't depend on anyone; but I can depend on HIM.
I've slept in places you would not go, and nothing's changed at all;
but what I know is I have faith to go where I am called.
I write in verse to encourage all who read that they receive;
that they would choose to move ahead, and prove what they believe.
My struggles are very real, my friends, but I'm encouraged too.
The words I write help me to live, to do the things I do.
I ask for prayers and nothing else, yet some folks want to help.
I appreciate the thoughts;
but if you can't, don't say you will; I'm not after what you've got.
I do depend on GOD for help. I'm not naked or unfed;

you know if I only depended on folks alone, I would now be dead.
GOD is good, HE has always been, and HE will always be;
I do appreciate you all, and I do hope that you see.
I have shared with you my heart of hearts in many different rhymes;
good things come for those who wait and mine will come in time.
This is what I know.

In God's Perfect Time

We wonder why things are this way, when
death comes knocking on our door.
She closed her eyes in GOD'S perfect time
and stepped through heaven's doors.
We feel that dying is a thing, those we will see no more.
The Bible says that angels sing, rejoicing when we arrive.
So death is just like being born. It's all GOD'S perfect time.

God Will Make a Way

Our GOD will make a way when there seems no way at all,
HE spoke, the tempest silenced, at the whisper of HIS call,
the winds became a gentle breeze, in the wonder of it all.
There is nothing—oh no, nothing—that our MIGHTY GOD don't know.
Are you ready for salvation? Drop that sin, just let it go.
There's forgiveness at the cross, of destiny and pain;
at a time your sins where washed, right along with guilt and shame.
Just remember, on the third day; HE arose, came back to life;
at that moment, it was finished, all is new, HE made it right.
What a love HE has for all, who in HIS image we are made,
So blessed and highly favored, we are children of the day.
We were first HIS enemy; HE says we now are friends,
joy for all eternity, a place where love will cease to end.
Taken up to heaven by HIS grace and through our faith.
There is one way not another; yes, our GOD made a WAY.
Children, listen to the whisper, the only ONE that is the WAY.
GOD has made a WAY where no other way can ever be,
HE'S the AUTHOR of our salvation, who commands our destiny.

Beautifully Broken

It took quite a while to chip at the stone;
my heart was so hardened; though, lost and alone.
I did not realize how much GOD loved me;
how in this dark state, HE would not let me be.
Abandoned by family, each door had been closed;
so I wandered around, till my heart became stone.
Angry that life could have taken such a turn;
my love had died, but I needed to learn.
Even when loved ones are taken away;
I found GOD'S love greater at the end of the day.
Beautifully broken is what I had become;
all by GOD'S grace and the blood of HIS SON.
Beauty for ashes and strength for my fears;
assurance that my GOD would always be here.
In all of my grief and my hardness of heart;
HE never once left me, not once did HE part.
The LORD, HE has given and has taken away;
I was broken in pieces, but at the end of the day;
HE has given me joy and a heart filled with hope;
but I had to be broken at the end of my rope.
JESUS suffered, died, and was risen again;
brought back to life and is the hope of all men.
Every woman and child, all girls and boys;
HE came as a light so that we might have joy.
A hope and a future for all who believed;
but we must be broken and fall to our knees.
I am beautifully broken, for my heart is brand new;
I was bought with a price, my friends, so were you.
It took all the love that our FATHER could give;

that blood on the cross had then made us HIS.
To cover our sins and to take away shame;
if we, by our faith, would call out HIS name.
The grace that HE'S given to all who'd believe;
is more than enough to save you and me.
It's okay to be broken; it's okay to weep;
life has its moments, but through it, we'll see;
the love of our FATHER, just how wide and how deep.
It's because HE so loved us, that we have been made new;
it's because HE is faithful, holy, and true.
It's because of our sin that HE suffered and died;
it's because HE is risen; we were given new life.

I Am What I Am

I am what I am, who GOD made me to be;
bought with a price, by HIS blood on that tree;
that cross gladly taken, a perfect pure lamb;
the grace of the ages, CHRIST the I AM.
HE said, "I am in the FATHER and the FATHER'S in me."
Two cannot walk together, unless they agree;
along with the SPIRIT, in complete unity.
I am who GOD made me, as unique as I am;
molded and shaped by the grace of HIS hands;
for HE is the POTTER and I am the clay;
I accept who I am, for HE made me this way.
HIS breath gave me life, as HIS grace gave me hope;
I was so broken, defeated, at the end of my rope.
Nowhere to turn to, and nowhere to run;
on my knees called to JESUS, put my faith in GOD'S SON.
HE said, "You will find me. Search with your whole heart."
"When I knock, let me in, and I'LL never depart."
"Just trust ME, my child. Hold on to my hand;
for you, there is hope; your future's my plan."
"I made you the way that you are; wait and see,
but heaven is different, for with ME you will be."
"I am what I am, for GOD made ME to be;
HIS child in heaven; joy eternally."

What I Found

I found my life, when I laid it down;
broken me upon the ground.
The tears I had not shed in years;
so lost, and needing to be found.
I found salvation, seeking love; a love not made by man;
I laid my life down at the cross; that's when GOD took my hand.
HE gave me faith so I'd believe, the plan HE has for me;
GOD found me in my brokenness, and said HE'D never leave.
I look at things, so differently; not like I did back then,
because my eyes are not the same; I have been born again.
I focus on the good that is, and all the good to come;
I have a future and a hope, given by GOD'S SON.
I have assurance in HIS WORD, that regardless how life is;
I know that HE will wipe my tears and I am always HIS.
I found life when I laid mine down, my worldly, selfish ways;
so now I focus on the good that I can see today.
but more than this, my treasure is in the place my heart will be;
the past no longer lives here, friend; it's
because I found what I believe.

Praise Him Anyway

I will praise HIM through my teardrops,
as I praise HIM in my smiles;
for no matter what may happen, HE is with me all the while.
At times HE walks beside me, as we stroll I give HIM praise;
but at times HE carries me, when life's storms get in my way;
and in the rain HE comforts me; I know I'll be okay.
It rains upon the good and bad; the sun shines on us all the same;
the difference is that when we praise HIM, whatever life may be;
when we always lift HIS holy name; we do more than just believe.
If we say that we believe and we live our lives by faith;
then we will praise HIM both in sunshine and also in the rain.
In every circumstance in life, no matter bad or good;
we should lift the NAME above all names;
and it must be understood.
HE is in control of everything; HIS ways are not our ways;
so regardless of what happens, praise HIM anyway!
How can we only love HIM when everything's okay?
When life is only sunshine and pain is far from view?
How can you only praise HIM when life is good to you?
But when bad times come we question
HIM; we murmur and complain;
we seem to think HE loves us less and refrain to praise HIS name.
We rebel against our MAKER for not getting our own ways.
I hope we learn this lesson, that regardless what we see;
regardless of emotions or how we feel life should be.
Regardless of our happiness or whether we are in pain.
Remember that GOD has got your back, so praise HIM anyway.

I Do Not Walk Alone

Psalm 16:11
I do not walk this path alone; l hold my FATHER'S hand;
HE knows the way I need to go; my journey is HIS plan.
HE leads me through the valley; by HIS love HE guides my way.
HE will take me to the mountaintop; in HIS love I choose to stay.
My faith is in HIS grace alone; where HE is, there I will be;
to walk with HIM and talk with HIM for all eternity.
I will not walk this path alone; my GOD is here with me;
and where the storms of life are found; there HE will also be.
HE has never ever left my side; HIS SPIRIT comforts me;
HE came to live within my heart for all eternity.

Words

Gracious words speak volumes and bitter words the same.
Grace can build and lift a life and never places blame;
but bitter words can make one fall and bring tears to your eyes;
they can destroy all hope within and cause a soul to die.
When children hear, "I love you and I'm so proud you're mine,"
it screams out adoration and can stand the test of time.
Those words will be remembered; I will guarantee it true;
so watch the words you speak, my friend; they will come back to you.
The Bible says we will be judged by every word we say;
I believe that it is true and there will come a day;
when we will stand before the throne of GOD to explain those words
    we said;
did our words bring life to someone or did they cause their death?
Unless you're saved and have confessed, and GOD in turn forgave,
unless you're born again, my friend, and your sins have all been paid.
Just like the woman brought to CHRIST; all sin forgiven for,
remember the words that JESUS spoke, "Go and sin no more."
If we are truly born again, and CHRIST in us abides;
there will be a change in us, with nothing more to hide.
Watch your words and think, my friend, before you say a thing;
and ask yourself, "If I should speak, what will my words bring?"

Your Heart Is Here with Me

Two waves on different oceans; how the tide will rise and call;
me looking at the morning light; you're looking at the sunset fall.
Your every moment on my mind, as I wait impatiently;
to kiss your lips and hold you tight, the day you're here with me.
Across the many miles, to a point our waves do meet,
floating ever gently, as a cool wind in the breeze.
My lady, you're my sunshine even in the rain.
Even through the storms I face, your love has eased my pain.
I was dying and alone; your love reached out to me;
across the many miles, beyond the vastness of the sea.
Your kindness drew me closer, as my love for you did bloom;
my loneliness had gone away, in my little empty room.
You gave me hope when hope was gone; sweet breath to come alive;
you didn't know the plan I had; and my desire to die.
GOD sent you as an angel to me, to save me from my plight;
but more than that, to love me back and hold me in the night.
You are my special angel, my love, way beyond the deep blue sea;
I'll never be lonely again, because your heart is here with me.

For my Beverly, *Mahal na mahal kita.*

You Don't Know What You Have

Until you've given all, you don't know what you've got;
until you've poured your heart and soul, you will feel that you have not.
Until you use the gift GOD gave and give that gift away;
you'll never know the beauty of the gift you could have gave.
GOD gave the very best HE had by the blood of HIS SON;
HE gave the world an awesome gift, as HIS will was being done.
CHRIST died but on the third day rose to life; our victory was won.
HE said we'd do much greater things, if only we believed;
I've got the very power of GOD living within me.
I've been forgiven of my every sin, and so I can forgive.
The love of GOD empowers me so that I long to give.
We don't know what we have, until the time we do;
when faith is put to action and our religion's true.
When GOD says we can do it, and we believe HIM then;
we will know just what we have, the love for GOD and man.
When we give this love away, we never lose a thing;
for it's in giving we receive, and prove the things we say.
It was at the gate of beautiful, not with silver or with gold;
the beggar received his miracle, such a gift he did behold.
To walk again and be made whole, is what he got that day;
but it took the want of a willing heart, to give that love away.

Only Passing Through

We are strangers in this world of yours, only passing through,
after all these years we are still not home, for we yet have much to do.
I'm that guy who you passed many times on the road of life behind;
I waved but you looked straight ahead; I was only being kind.
I'm that person who had shown you love as I opened up your door
and let you go ahead of me so many times before.
You never said a single word; you wouldn't look me in the eye.
You'd never guessed I prayed for you, for your very soul I cried.
We are the children on your TV sets, with flies upon our face.
Dirty and hungry yet you see us smile; we have learned to take our
    place.
You changed your channel quickly, for you dared not see the truth;
but it's okay, we still can smile, we were only passing through.
We are the children who were never born to live out one single day
and wondered why the world of yours was such a selfish place.
Minds are changed in an instant, and like trash we were tossed away.
We could have been your children, but you sent us home that day.
We are sorry if we did anything to help you change your view;
but we are home with JESUS; we were only passing through.
I'm the lady with the shopping cart filled with things I've found,
I'm hungry and I'm homeless, and you don't want me around.
There is no place for me down here, but I do what I must do.
For me, it's temporary, because I'm only passing through.
I'm the man in church with love for you, as I share what I have found.
I was headed to a burning hell, until JESUS turned my life around.
I tell of how that old life was, in a drunken, drug-filled rage;
I heard my SAVIOR call; when I answered, my life was changed.
I've been slapped and I've been spit upon, but my love remains the
    same.

We are strangers in this world of yours, sojourners you could say.
Headed for our heavenly home, which no man can take away;
there are many more like us down here, but we yet have much to do.
We live our lives by faith through prayers; we are only passing through.

More about Words

While pondering so many things on this journey that I take;
I have heard so many words, which I hear people say.
Some words of love; but very few, have happened on my ears;
but other words have hurt my heart, and often brought me tears.
Words are how we live this life; those things of which we say;
they reveal our heart of hearts, our hurts, our doubts, our faith.
They can bring peace and comfort, or they can cause strife and war;
they can build up or destroy a life; and oh, friends, so much more.
When we speak the words of GOD, and believe what HE would say;
we speak words that come alive and we're better off that way.
The Bible says we will be judged by every idle word we say.
I've seen two different children, two different kinds of lives;
to one, was spoken grace and love; to the other, words despised.
The one grew up to love others and self; the second believed the lies.
One would succeed by leaps and bounds; the other fell along the way;
he accepted all the doubtful words and repeated what they'd say.
(So before you say a single word, think of what those words convey;
remember we are responsible for every word we say).
The tongue is such a little thing, but the damage it can do;
that raging fire it ignites, can be because of you.
We can control this tongue of ours, if we think before we speak.
"Will this bring GOD the glory, or to my pride, relief?"
"Will what I speak bring grace and love to someone along the way?"
"Will it show the world who lives inside, the ONE I say I praise?"
Gentle words can calm a storm or cause a fire to blaze.

I Called It Mine

Twenty-four hours in a day, seven days a week.
We each are given the exact same time, to choose, to dream, to be.
When I think about this time I have, when I truly ponder, "Why?"
I realize I've wasted so much, of this thing called time.
Where have all the years gone? Just where did they all go?
I still remember seventeen, so quickly I've grown old.
Life is but a breath, my friend, when compared to eternity:
when I think about what I did with mine, it's still hard to believe.
Each minute that I've wasted, not spent on someone else,
was when I got greedy, and spent it on myself.
Of all the good I could have done, I thought of only me.
I was more important than someone else's dreams.
We wonder why we are here on earth; where are we in this plan?
I have found the answer simple—to love GOD first and then our
    fellow man.
It matters not the sexes when someone needs a hand.
You see, love is being practical, an action verb; it's true,
what we say means so much less than what we really do.
I called things mine, but are they? If I really think this through,
I find that things are loaned to me to see what I will do.
Will I then hoard these things I get, and covet everyone,
or will I give to meet a need when the day is done?
Will I honor GOD or things, is the thought that comes along,
to know to do good and not do it, friend, definitely is wrong.
So with a deep conviction, and a strong desire to love;
I have learned what's more important; it is GOD I need to trust.
In giving we are getting, where our treasures are we'll be,
earth is but a testing ground for all eternity.
I used to call what I had mine, until I lost it all;

it opened up my eyes to know, pride comes before a fall.
You see, GOD so loved the world, HE gave HIS very best;
HE gave so that we might be saved, my friends (you know the rest).
That blood shed on that cross of grace can save all who believe,
call out HIS name, HE promises that HE would never leave.
I called things mine and wasted time, now I'm getting gray,
I've learned that life can come and go so quickly day by day.
I've learned that joy is something you get when you give love away,
and happiness are happenings we don't get every day.
I've learned that GOD loves me so much that HE gave HIS only Son;
when JESUS died and rose to life, the victory was won.
This age has taught me many things, which youth could never do;
it's better that I come in last, you see; this is the truth.
Without the pride I had before, I'm humbled in this life;
joy is loving GOD, then you; that's how it's all made right.
To give is better than to receive, when all is done and said,
by loving you, I love me too, and choose life instead of death.
I had it all and lost it all, with sadness over time;
but now with joy, I give away those things that are not mine.

Love His Way

A child is born, by a virgin birthed;
for thirty-three years he would walk the earth;
this SON of GOD, the LIGHT of man;
but darkness did not understand.
That he would die; his blood was shed;
to save all those who would bow their heads.
Those who would believe GOD'S grace;
and that he chose to take our place.
HE did it for the human race.
HE first turned water into wine;
he healed the sick, opened blind eyes.
HE came to set the captives free;
and that includes both you and me.
How can some say, they don't believe;
there's no excuse; just look around, and you will see;
the world around you proves HIS love;
but many say; "It's not enough."
They choose their ways, they do walk blind;
they've chosen just to close their eyes.
They have ears, but will not hear;
they cannot know, who they won't fear.
Loving sin, they live by night;
they do not understand the LIGHT.
How can they know, until they come?
Repented, bowed, before GOD'S SON.
HE came to be the ONLY WAY;
to make us see the light of day.
To adopt us as HIS children of light;
and free us from the blinding night.

But many feel that they are saved;
but never rose from sin's dark grave.
The ten commandments that HE gave;
they do not choose; to them, obey.
Love the LORD, and have no other,
and truly choose to love your brothers.
If we would choose to seek HIS face;
all the rest will fall in place.
Respect and honor are due to HIM;
fear the ONE who died for sin;
kiss the SON and praise HIS name;
believe and so you walk by faith.
Obey and choose to love HIS way.

One Seed Is Enough

A tiny seed fell and it started to grow;
it fell through the cracks so that no one would know.
The pain and the fear of that life of abuse;
just reminders of the ways of my youth.
They called me a liar, when I told them the truth.
Always so frightened that in life I would see;
more of those teardrops, which started to bleed.
Memories so deep that I wanted to die,
I had shed so much sadness, my tears started to dry.
Grown up so quickly, if only they knew;
that the seed of the gospel, at fourteen, also grew.
life was not easy when you have PTSD;
as if inside, a war, what a mind can believe.
Feeling so worthless, without hope at all;
It would be many years, when I answered the call.
Stumbling through life, all my innocence, lost;
I did not hope to live;
but that one little seed had now started to give.
It cut through the stone of a once-frozen start,
and gave me new birth, as it transformed my heart.
That seed that was planted so long ago,
by the love of my FATHER, that gift I would know.
The words of a journey that grew with one seed;
who fell through the cracks, now a mighty oak tree.
My story had sadness, but much joy in the end;
always be hopeful, and trust JESUS, my friends.
Encourage each other and spread all that love;
we must never forget that one seed is enough.

The Open Door

In my hardheaded pride, I was blind, couldn't see;
the fool in the mirror the whole time, was me.
I thought I had friends, who would be there, you see;
but they scattered away, like leaves on a breeze.
I thought that I knew all that could ever be known;
so blind by pride, did it all on my own.
I didn't need help, or so I had thought;
brought to my knees, and convicted by GOD.
By faith I was saved, by the grace of HIS blood;
when HE hung on that cross, just one drop was enough.
HE suffered and died such a horrible death;
but on the third day, well, you know the rest.
The good news is salvation, through the blood that HE shed;
HE arose from the tomb, though they witnessed HIM dead.
JESUS was born as a man on this earth;
born destined to die, to give us new birth.
More precious than diamonds, more treasured than gold;
we were bought by HIS blood; yes, a gift to behold.
This door is left open that no one can shut;
but one must be broken, and in want of HIS touch.
Repent of your ways as you enter by faith;
The door? This same JESUS, who arose from grave.
I once had the world, but it all was a lie;
I'm made born again, but I too had to die;
die to the flesh and believe on the Son.
HE told us back then that HIS grace was enough.
When I entered the door to the hope which HE gave;

I had to believe, there was only ONE WAY.
ONE WAY to the FATHER in heaven above;
JESUS, the LAMB, the true gift of GOD'S love.

This Sea

This sea can't separate, the way that this love is;
those waves can't say a thing, about the outcome of a love as this.
Those waves can't crash upon our dreams, or harm this love of ours;
for you see, my heart believes, it's written in the stars.
This ocean in its vastness, regardless of how deep;
can't disregard my beating heart, and the love it wants to keep.
And every storm that comes our way, regardless of its rage;
can't keep apart two beating hearts, for GOD will make a way.
The day I asked you to be mine, the day you said, "I will";
I knew we would be faithful to this love, and we are faithful still.
The sea can't come between a love that's meant to be;
I pray and wait until the day, that day you're here with me.
Between the faith we have in GOD, and this love so true;
this sea can never tear apart, the love I have for you.

Because You Believed

Dark and alarming, this storm on the rise;
nothing else like it, was formed in the skies.
The rushing of winds, at this end of time;
darker than this, there are none else to find.
When the end of this earth will finally unwind.
They did not want the truth, the light of the LAMB, or the blessings
    HE gave;
though the light of the world had shown on their face;
they were more satisfied with death and the grave.
Rejecting the love of the BEGOTTEN of GOD,
they chose to walk without light;
not wanting to hear HIM, they rejected HIS life.
This terrible fire will destroy and consume;
cry out to JESUS, for HE so loved you.
HE proved it by HIS blood, which lead to HIS death,
but on the third day HE rose, back with life in HIS breath.
The LORD of all glory, always was and will be;
LORD of all LORDS and the KING of all kings;
the redeemed and all evil will all bow their knees.
Many are called, but chosen are few;
grace mixed with faith, and the love that you do.
At the end of the day, it's all up to you.
That storm is approaching; there is little time left;
to cry out to JESUS, for the life of HIS breath.
Believing in hope, when all hope seemed but gone;
is a love that forever, will go on and on.
There is still hope for heaven, for GOD had a plan;
to save all the world, HE became a man;
who suffered and died on that cross on skull hill;

HE gave us HIS grace, and it's here with us still.
Born of the FATHER, a perfect pure lamb;
our salvation, JESUS, who is called the I AM.
We as in the garden of Adam and Eve;
must also choose: to doubt or to believe.
To trust and obey our GOD out of love;
believe that the blood of HIS grace is enough.
By love, I have warned you, you who have read this rhyme;
that soon HE will be here; there is so little time;
in a flash, like a thief in the darkness of night,
and that darkness will fall as a raven in flight.
For those who have chosen to follow the light;
who share the true gospel by the fruit of their lives.
Those who rejected the lies for the truth;
children of light, by love that you do;
all the splendor of heaven given to you.
You believed on HIS grace and the WORD of HIS TRUTH.

Jesus, the Door of Life

Come into the door, the river of life;
the beautiful splendor, just after we die.
The door to our future, the hope of a day,
When HE and HIS angels will take us away.
Come in and receive, of the fullness of HIM;
JESUS, ETERNAL, CREATOR, I AM.
Come into the supper prepared just for you,
the grace that HE gave, the blood our sins drew,
to save us from death, believe in the ONE;
who first gave us HIS breath; we have only begun.
Encourage each other; there is coming a time;
when we will be changed in a blink of an eye;
a gathering of children to meet in the sky.
Hold on to the promise; by faith, you will know;
cleave to HIS love; HE is not letting go.
HE is the river of life; there is only one;
we can't get to heaven without faith in the SON.
The doorway is open, for whosoever will come;
by faith in believing in JESUS, GOD'S SON.
The journey began, when called by HIS grace;
we believed and encountered the start,
for GOD so love the world that HE gave;
HE gave us the key to the door of HIS heart.

Rain Dancers

Storms in life will come our way;
for even flowers need the rain;
there can't be sunshine without pain;
but better days will come our way.
GOD made roses, fragrant things,
oh, the joy that they can bring;
so beautiful, their colors bloom;
that awesome odor fills the room.
As wonderful as they can be,
they still bear thorns that make you bleed.
They can cause pain; we can agree.
Just like the storms we face in life;
the tears we shed when life's not right;
our countenance can change that fast;
when clouds are gray, with hearts downcast.
But I have found a different way;
to look at life when skies are gray;
I dance when raindrops come my way;
and smile at what my GOD will say.
"Fear not, my child. I'm here with you;
for storms must come, but as they do;
remember that my WORD is truth;
I'm never letting go of you."
Dance in the rain; you'll be okay;
the sun will shine another day;
but until then, believe and pray;
Our GOD is faithful to make a way.

Be rain dancers, and as you do;
you'll have a different attitude;
you'll learn to trust as you obey;
and through it all, you'll be okay.

Will They Listen?

They will not listen; it's hard to hear,
when worldly noise, has shut their ears,
when what they see, does not please GOD;
I find their wording rather odd.
I hear what their tongues have to say;
those curses thrown in casual ways.
our words will be judged by HIM one day.
They will not listen through the doubt;
to study, to show, to know what GOD'S WORD is about.
Believing everything men say; and not for themselves, finding out.
It's hard to hear when GOD will speak,
when with their pride, the flesh is weak.
The SPIRIT is willing to show the way;
when pride of man is cast aside;
but they in darkness live a lie,
of sin and doubt, they cannot hide.
They say, "I'm born again like you,"
though, through their actions, prove untrue.
A tree is so judged by its fruit.
Repentance comes when your heart breaks;
when sin abounds, so more GOD'S grace.
HE longs to see the whole world saved,
that none shall perish in the way.
HE says, "Repent! Why be destroyed?
Change your mind, your heart, will too;
Believe in ME, the WAY and TRUTH."
"Children, come to life and see,
your lives will change when you follow ME."
"Will you listen to what I say?"

"And will you now cry out MY name?"
"Will you be MY child of day?"
"Repent right now, and walk MY WAY."

Not Without Understanding

So many things in living are hard to understand
so is the same with dying, they both go hand in hand.
I sought for understanding, you see I'd lost my way,
I walked the city streets, damp from winter rain;
weeping uncontrollably, broken by my pain.
In prayer to the holy ONE, whose love will not refrain,
my answer found in CHRIST alone, who gently called my name.
My faith aloft on angel's wings, on GOD I can rely
HE swiftly carries me above the reasons that I cry.
Of all the things I understand, and the many things I don't;
I know that I can never quit or ever give up hope.
Believe me when I say that I can walk upon the sea,
for greater things I'll surely do; HE lives inside of me.
HIS WORD has made me come to life; I was dead in all my sin,
I believe HIS love for me, HE died but rose again.
I believe HE saved me from a hell that was my own
and I believed that from then on, I would never be alone.
It's not without understanding that I write this rhyme you read,
I pray you find encouragement, that by your faith believe.
HIS blood, the wine, once shed for us upon that cursed tree;
HIS body, torn, the bread of life for all who would believe.
JESUS CHRIST, the SON of GOD, through HIM GOD'S grace
    abounds,
believe and trust HIS love for us, for that's where life is found.
Let HIS love permeate your soul, your very inner being,
do what HE says then move ahead; do more than just believe.
HE gives understanding, HIS wisdom knows no bounds,
FATHER'S always faithful; that's where HIS love is found.
Upon a cruel and lonely cross, HIS blood was shed for you

to take away the sin you bear, to make you bright and new.
HE is the only WAY to GOD, our FATHER on HIS throne,
the only saving WAY to GOD, found in HIS SON and by HIS
   blood atoned.

Brokenness

I thought that I knew everything, in the foolishness of youth;
and didn't want to listen, to logic or to truth.
I was indestructible, so full of worldly pride,
I did all I did for me; my sin, I did not hide.
I thought I was a leader, that the world would follow me;
that was not my case in life; I was the follower, you see.
If I could live through youth again, and know what I know now;
life would have been so different then; for you see, I've learned to bow.
In brokenness, upon my knees, I saw what I became;
I saw how much I needed GOD, so alas, I called HIS name.
I lost so much, with all that pride, those many wasted years;
my GOD so loved me, this I found; HE let me shed those tears.
HE allowed my tears in life, to break my lofty pride;
repented to a change of mind, the day HE came inside.
A whole new different person, is who I have become;
first broken, then made new again, by faith in GOD'S own SON.
Who shed HIS precious blood for me, to wash my sins away.
And the best thing I have learned in life, is that I need HIM every day.
So brokenness is never bad, if it brings you to your knees;
and turns you into someone who, you were always meant to be.

Godly sorrow brings repentance that leads to salvation, but worldly sorrow brings death. (2 Cor. 7:10)

The City

HE looked upon the city, in the misty morning haze,
and much to his amazement, it was now the end of days.
The wars we fought on distant shores could not compare to this,
a twinkle in the eye of time (as life), only a mist.
HE pondered as he studied, as he knew this day would come,
that moment when he'd see the face of JESUS, GOD'S own SON.
In the twinkle of an eye, just like that, brand new;
that moment life forever changed, your every hope came true.
It's not because you did something, which caused you to be saved;
but by your faith your heart was changed, by GOD'S amazing grace.

Praise GOD for That Day

So brokenness is never bad if it brings you to your knees;
and turns you into someone, who you were always meant to be.
With a smile on your face, you now walk toward the beam;
feeling safe and secure, now awake from the dream.
That nightmare now gone, as you finely draw breath:
now safe and secure, in a warm place of rest.
Now remember your life as it was way back when;
you stumbled in darkness, again and again.
With nowhere to run and fear on all sides;
you would not bow to GOD, all because of your pride.
So you lived as the world; and did all you could do;
a heart set on destruction, for you had not a clue.
Until one day GOD'S mercy introduced you to grace;
HE called you from death, and put life in its place.
It's when you saw the LIGHT of the world, the WAY;
you were made new; with your darkness, now day.
JESUS would call you, and you then heard HIS voice;
but to answer or not, you were given a choice.
By faith you believed in the grace that HE gave;
free from your sin, far from death and the grave.
Now imagine that lighthouse again, one last time;
and praise GOD for that day, you were brought back to life.
Imagine a lighthouse on the darkest of nights, a beacon of hope
when your life was not right.
With a smile on your face you now sail toward the beam, feeling
safe and secure now awake from your dream.
The nightmare now gone as you finally draw breath, secure in
reality, in your warm place of rest.
Now remember your life as if was way back when, as you

stumbled in darkness again and again. With nowhere to run and fear on all sides, you would not bow to GOD all because of your pride.
So you lived as the world, did all you could do, a heart bent on destruction though you had not a clue, but when you saw the LIGHT of the World, the WAY, you where then made new and the dark turned to day. JESUS called and you heard HIS voice, but to answer or not, you were given a choice.
By faith you believed in the grace which HE gave, free from your sin far from death and the grave. Now imagine that lighthouse again; one last time, and praise GOD for that day you were brought back to life.

All of the Above

Have *hope* that all will turn out right; there will be day after this night;
the tears will dry and joy will come, along with morning light.
Have *faith* that GOD will see you through; HE'S made a WAY;
HE is the TRUTH, HE has better plans for you; call out to HIM, HIS heart is true.
Peace HE brings to those in need, whose hearts cry out to HIM,
repent of doubt, the very thing, which often leads to sin.
Love the ONE who first loved you, who died upon that tree,
hold on to the WAY, the TRUTH, who died for you and me.
Believe HE is the ONLY WAY, and for you HE died;
but on the third day much had changed, for HE came back to life.
Trust HIM for HE'S coming back, so do all that is above;
JESUS CHRIST, the ONLY WAY, for our GOD so loved.

Jesus, Light of the World

The LIGHT shined in the darkness, though man could not comprehend;
the CREATOR of the world would become flesh, and live as one of them.
Born of the Virgin Mary, HE slept on a bed made of straw;
in a manger the sleeping baby, would grow to die for us all.
JESUS, born of the SPIRIT, GOD'S only BEGOTTEN SON;
the LIGHT, the WAY to the FATHER, our SAVIOR, the ONLY ONE.
For thirty-three years HE walked the earth, sinless in all HIS ways;
the perfect pure LAMB of the FATHER, this was the ONLY WAY.
Without the shedding of blood, there is no remission for sin;
so it took HIS blood on that cross on skull hill to forgive; it would take HIM.
The tearing of flesh HE endured all for us;
the nails that pierced HIS feet and HIS hands,
the pain that HE took as HIS FATHER turned away;
was more than HE could stand.
HE said, "It is finished," as HE bowed HIS head;
at that moment, HE died in our stead.
In a borrowed tomb, they lay HIM, but friend it was not the end!
On the third day, HE rose from death, alive in the sight of men.
The victory won from the death of that cross, all for the love of mankind;
this same JESUS who walked on the earth, who calmed the sea and opened blind eyes.
This grace which HE gave to a world so lost, this light sent from GOD to mankind.

So call out to HIM and in your brokenness see, as your eyes open to TRUTH;
by faith, you are saved for HE rose from the grave; believe that HE did it for you.

The Fire

HE lit a fire within me that burns so strong and clear,
I heard HIS soft voice calling me; it was when my heart drew near.
I heard the good news of HIS love upon Golgotha tree;
HE shed HIS blood because of love, to save the lost like me.
HIS love for me is more than I can understand,
HE didn't scream or curse at me, just said to take HIS hand.
That HE would wipe my tears away, and hold me through the storms;
that HE would never leave me, and HIS love would keep me warm.
I love my GOD, my LORD, and KING because HE first loved me;
it was HE who called my name and caused me to believe.
This journey that I've walked in life is not the same as yours
but we have had our share of tears, For when it rains, sometimes it pours.
To suffer and die for the sins of man is the reason why HE came;
Repent, my friend, in brokenness and humbly call HIS name.
HE will light a fire in your heart; you'll want others to be saved,
praise the ONE who died for you, who has risen from the grave.

We Hurt the Ones We Love

It seems to me that when I cry, when tears flow from my eyes,
they are because of those I love; it's then I realize;
the pain which causes them to fall is because I love so much;
it seems that when I've lost control, my heart breaks by their touch.
Those times we are misunderstood, when we misunderstand;
it runs both ways and anger flies, the two go hand in hand.
As words are freely tossed around, we become so unaware,
we forget that deep inside, we really love and care.
Pride at times just blinds our eyes; it just will not give in
and so we feel that we must fight, that it's our turn to win.
We seem to hurt the ones we love, but why? It shouldn't be!
Because the ones we love are those, the ones we truly need.
I've learned a lesson in my life, which brought me to my knees;
as I confessed my foolish pride, I cried out,
"FATHER, please forgive me for this way I feel. I knew it should not be."
You see, I hurt the girl I love so much; it broke her heart,
I should have thought to realize just how much that she loved me.
Before we misunderstand a thing, that can tear our love apart;
we must consider not our own, but another's heart.
Before you hurt the ones you love, just think before you speak,
and pray that GOD will make a way; that our love still can be.
For we can lose the ones we love, by what we do or say,
and they may not return to us when our pride gets in the way.
"I'm so sorry that I hurt you, love. Please do not love me less."
"Forgive me for the way I get, for with you I'm truly blessed."
"I did not mean to break your heart and believe me I will try;
to nevermore cause you to hurt or ever make you cry."

He Loved Us First

For GOD so loved the world, that to us HE gave HIS SON,
the only perfect LAMB of GOD that was; HE was the only ONE.
To be a ransom for us all, by HIS death upon that cross;
you see, my friends, it was HIS call, to seek and save the lost.
As we bow our heads before HIM, the KING above all kings,
we must be humbly broken, and to HIM must take a knee.
HE calls us in our brokenness; in HIS grace, we can believe,
that GOD so love the world so much, how HE loves you and me.
HE loved us first before we knew, HIS love for us could be,
and that is why HE sent HIS SON to die for you and me.
HE took the stripes upon HIS back and nails through hands and feet,
buried in a borrowed tomb—HIS? No, that could never be.
For in three days HE rose to life; HE won the victory!
And by it saved both you and I; now death has lost its sting.
Do you accept this gift HE gives, which cannot be bought or sold?
Do you believe HIS grace by faith is worth much more than gold?
Can you take up your cross for HIM? And do as HE has said?
Will you study the WORD HE gives, and put your flesh to death?
Those sins that seem to hold you down, no longer have control;
because the blood HE shed for us, has said to let them go.
All praises to our GOD above! So worthy is HIS name,
HE is the ONE who first loved us, before all things were framed.
HE is the ONE that we must love and then our fellow man,
point them to Golgotha cross; they will soon understand.
HIS SPIRIT will help them know the TRUTH, the LIGHT who
    guides their way;
and you, by love, have done GOD'S will, at the end of this new day.

True Love

I love you just the way you are. Love, please don't ever change;
it's what's inside that really counts; that's what matters anyway.
True love accept us as we are, that we can make mistakes;
it's your heart I feel in love with then; I pray it will never change.
You are kind and show affection; you are humble in your ways,
you love GOD; that is perfection, unafraid to give HIM praise.
That is what I love about you; that's the reason you are mine;
for your heart reached out to touch me, at a perfectly needed time.
I was numb from that depression, which attacked my heart and mind;
because your heart reached out to me that day, you truly saved my
     life.
You didn't even know me, but you knew I was in pain;
you chose to take a chance on me, to love me anyway.
It seemed that no one cared about all I was going through;
but GOD had sent an angel; I knew then 'cause then came you.
You never asked; you only gave me reason to want to live,
I was so deep in sorrow, yet I smiled in spite of it.
I tried to hide the sadness to erase the memories
but my heart became so hard that I would not get on my knees.
Oh, I was far from perfect, but you didn't even care;
all I knew I needed someone; it was you who GOD put there.
Over time, we'd gotten closer; how we laughed and how we cried;
together yet so far apart, grew this love, this bond, with time.
Though the distance separates us, this love so meant to be;
you still remained my angel, far across the deep blue sea.
And no, I'm still not perfect, but with you I long to try;
I want to be the kind of man, who sees not from my eyes.
I long to see things from my soul, my very inner being,
just exactly like the very time that your soul saw me.

I was someone I thought unlovable—homeless, falling apart,
it took a love that's oh so rare, to mend my broken heart.
You never asked me for a thing that many would have done,
but you did do what was asked of you by JESUS, GOD'S own SON.
You reached out over the many miles, across the vastness of the sea,
you touched a very broken heart, which caused me to believe.
I saw hope beyond all hope, a love so warm and true;
you see, my love, I found true love, that day that I found you.
The years have come and gone so fast, yet you are still with me,
we are within each other's hearts, divided by the sea.
Our life has changed in many ways; GOD'S blessed this bond that's
 true,
we made a choice and chose to love, not in words but what we do.
We found true love, a love which grows as each day passes by.
How it will end? GOD only knows, though we're both willing to try.
We do agree in prayer to GOD, that HIS perfect will be done;
my love, we are not perfect, yet there are many battles to be won.
We make mistakes as all will do; I know I've done my share,
with true love, we hold our faith; we know our GOD is always here.
Our GOD will make a way for us, a way we cannot see;
for by HIS grace, HE will see us through.
I know one day you'll be with me; it's because our love is true.
For Beverly, we have both made mistakes in life;
but I still want to be your husband, and I still want you to be my wife.

Mahal kita, always.
Love, your Mike.

We'll Get Through This Together

Take my hand; I'll help you, encourage you to try
we will get through this together, but it will take you and I.
This journey that we travel has bumps along the way
there will be joy and sorrow, tears in both night and day.
Together, we will make it, for GOD says we are one
united by the love we have, and led by GOD'S own SON.
We married not with paper, or all that manmade stuff
who GOD has joined together, will always be enough.
We are one united, for our love was meant to be
even when divided, by the distance of the sea.
You still can take my hand, my love, for it flows within my heart
and time will never change that, for by faith it does impart.
No matter what the outcome, I will still be here for you
for true love are not the words we say, but the actions that we do.
No matter what may happen, love, I will be right here for you
and we'll get through it together, because I know our love is true.
I realized you loved me from the very start, for you reached out
from the distance when you came inside my heart.
I asked you to be with me, to be my loving wife
when you said yes you sealed the deal, and that meant all our life.
We serve our LORD together, for together we will be
our love can't be divided, by the distance of the sea.

For my Beverly.

The Missing Piece

So much had happened in my youth, I didn't comprehend,
growing up was not so fun, so I would just pretend;
that life was just a fairy tale, my pain was not for real;
that I was loved and worthy of the peace that I would feel.
That my scars were won in battles that I fought;
the evil that I would conquer; I pretended I was loved.
A little boy so frightened inside a closet by himself,
that darkness brought on nightmares, for he knew nothing else.
Then other things had happened; I was afraid to say;
so I would just imagine, I knew no other way.
To survive was all that mattered; as I grew, the fear remained;
my future all but shattered, for I thought myself insane.
Drugs were introduced to me, at a young and tender age;
later attempts at suicide, that turned another page.
I didn't see a future, nor was hope within my heart;
but I knew something was missing, from the very start.
I was told that I was nothing, and that no one would love me,
without self-worth I cowered, and so I just believed.
I believed the lies that evil told, convinced the fault was mine;
so I carried guilt and brokenness, which took its toll with time.
I found love was that missing piece, a void I could not fill,
but I didn't know what true love was; for me, it wasn't real.
I grew to wonder many things, but mostly where to find,
this longing deep within my soul, said that this love could be mine.
One day someone spoke of JESUS, and that GOD so loved mankind,
they said HE bled and died for me, and that this love could be mine.
They said by faith I could believe the grace, the love HE gives;
they told me then that "GOD is LOVE," and that HE would make
   me HIS.

When I believed I found that thing, that missing part of me;
that void I tried to fill myself, I couldn't set me free.
HE set me free, but it took time, to mend my shattered heart;
but HE never left my side, from that very start.
I grew to know and trust my GOD; HIS WORD became my light,
HE took me from that darkness, those memories in my mind.
When CHRIST said, "It is finished," as HE died for you and me;
you see, it was the beginning, of what would set us free.
They buried HIM in a borrowed tomb, and sealed it with a stone,
HE died so that we could believe that GOD would make a WAY;
for after three days, HE rose to life, and turned our darkness into day.
So here I stand with joy to say, "HE'S filled the void in me."
HE is the WAY, the TRUTH, and LIFE; it's HE who set us free.
HE is that piece I needed most, to fill me from inside;
JESUS washed my sins away, and made my dark heart white.
So don't give up; do not return, to that dark place you once knew;
stand up and fight to do what's right, and to our GOD be true.

His Will

"THY will be done," the prayer goes; it is as HE allows,
our sovereign GOD has made a plan, perfect, as HE knows how.
We think our journeys in our hands and so we plan ahead,
but we don't know what it will bring, for tomorrow we may be dead.
Or we could live till ninety-eight, our GOD will surely show,
so we should say, "If GOD allows"; it's only HE who knows.
Don't get me wrong, it's okay to plan, to want the things we do;
but you must think, will it honor HIM, or is it all for you?
Do those desires of which we seek bring glory to the ONE,
who gave us grace and proved HIS love by giving us HIS SON?
Do we desire sinful things of which the world lusts?
Money, fame to praise our name, or is it in HIM we trust?
HE makes ways we cannot see, when we pray in faith;
when we choose to do HIS will, I know HE will make a way.
HIS will is so much better for HE has a better plan;
give it to HIM in prayer, then just leave it in HIS hands.
Ask for a vision when you pray, and when HE gives it to you;
run with it with all your might, and to your GOD be true.
HIS will be done in heaven and earth, as HE gives us daily bread;
trust in the ONE, the ONLY ONE, who knows what lies ahead.

It's Almost Time

This world is getting darker as sin just has its way;
we see it by what people do, the views which they convey.
They see many ways to heaven, although GOD says there's ONE,
it's believing in the cross of CHRIST, the shed blood of HIS own SON.
It's nearly time to go now; HE is coming back real soon;
it's not so much the things we say, but the love we do.
To love our GOD with all our hearts, and love our fellow man;
the words we say and things we do, should both go hand in hand.
To pray for the unlovable, who hate the way we are;
to love the sinner and hate the sin; yes, it can be very hard.
But the two must be separated; if this we do not do,
If we make the final judgment, we do not walk in the TRUTH.
Do we step up to feed the hungry? Do we cloth the one's in need?
Do we visit those in prison, as we set the captives free?
Is it our cross we carry, as we follow HIS command?
Do we make disciples of the lost as we lend a helping hand?
To be the heart of JESUS, to a world that soon will fade,
to truly love the ones HE loves, at the end of every day.
To humbly wash the feet and chose to be servant of all;
to be HIS hands and feet, and do as HE commands and calls.
To preach the good news of HIS love, and point them to the cross,
of the ONE who came, to seek and save the lost.
Church, HE'S coming very soon, so keep your candles lit;
let our lights shine within the dark and love in spite of it.

Don't Believe the Devil

Do not believe the devil, if bad news comes your way;
remember GOD has told you, that great things come by faith.
You see HE never changes, for HE remains the same;
call out in your sorrow, for HE will make a way;
miracles do happen; we see them every day.
Do not believe the enemy; he cannot tell the truth;
he lies and steals and murders, and could care less for you.
Folks say so many things, believing in their doubt;
oh they of little faith put in, getting little out.
The words they say are lifeless; they are not based on solid truth;
for fear has taken many, who don't believe what GOD can do.
Believe all things are possible; don't you ever doubt GOD can;
trust HIM as you pray in faith, and leave it in HIS hands.
HE makes ways that we can't see, as HE straightens crooked roads;
HE lightens heavy burdens, so many overloads.
HE is gracious in HIS giving, so trust the ONE who knows;
but remember HE is sovereign; that's just the way it goes.
"FATHER, if you're willing, take away this fear;
I know that you have got this too, for you are more than near."
"Your children will face trials along their journey's way;
show them you've not left them, but they need to walk by faith."
The devil is a liar! As are his minions too.
It's only GOD who loves you; HE has not abandoned you;
remember HE is faithful, and always will be TRUE.
You may feel like you're a failure, as you bow your head in shame,
but, my friend, it isn't over, just believe on JESUS'S name.

HE will change your circumstances, for your journey is HIS plan;
trust HIM, HE holds tomorrow; HE'S got the whole world in HIS hands.
Have faith just like a child; for you see, in truth you are;
hold on to the hope you have; HIS grace can take you far.

For All Mothers

There is a place where I can go, a time where I knew joy,
when Mama held me in her arms, protected from life's noise.
I loved my mama oh, so much, for I knew that she loved me;
and even though she's long been gone, this love I know won't leave.
The sacrifices that she made, to keep me fed and clothed,
she comforted my hurt and felt my pain; what she went through,
    GOD only knows.
There is that special place I go, a place within my mind;
that only her and I came be, a memory in frozen time.
Without mothers in this world, we couldn't know such love,
they are the ones who cared for us, though they need not be of blood.
Even if they adopted us and chose us specially,
the peace which comes from a mother's love, is something we all need.
Today is Mother's Day on earth, a time to give them praise.
We thank you, every mom, in our own special way.
Sometimes with flowers and a kiss, a card so you can know,
the love we have for you right now, that time will not let go.
Those moments when you held us close, the love we needed then;
are memories we cherish now, that will never have an end.

Dedicated to my mother, Alice, who went to be with JESUS, and to my adopted mama, Betty D. Renner. So grateful GOD gave us each other.

Come, Follow Me

Before time began HE had you on HIS mind;
HE loved you first way before there was time.
HE created all things, all that our eyes see;
the mountains and forest, every fish in the sea.
The eagles which soar and the sparrows that sing;
sparkling rivers that flow, the storms and the breeze.
HE came down to the earth to be born a man;
to die on a cross, a perfect pure LAMB.
Without the shedding of blood, there would be no remission for sin;
there was no other way; it had to be HIM.
As you know HE was born the LIGHT, we would find;
HE calmed the sea, and HE opened blind eyes,
HE chose to die for the sins of mankind.
HE rose from the dead as HE said that HE would;
so we could be free; yes, our FATHER is good.
HE said, "Take up your cross, all you who believe;
I'll be with you forever. Come, follow me."
So repent and be broken, we must be born anew;
forget the excuses of the bad which you do.
Our FATHER wants those, who will choose to do right;
who worship in spirit and truth by HIS might;
children who walk by the day, not by night.
Come follow JESUS, who won't lead us astray;
The TRUTH and the LIFE, the ONLY WAY.
To a place HE'S prepared, our heavenly home;
where no wars will be and sin cannot come in, joy unbelievable;
where tears will not flow.
HE said, "Oh, how I love you. With ME, you can be;
let go of the world, and come, follow me."

It's Okay

It's okay if I have no legs to move myself around;
I was not made to run and play; but it's okay, I've found.
I don't need legs to have a heart, to love the way I do;
for I can say that without legs, I'm still the same as you.
It's okay if I have no eyes to see the way you see;
I've never really needed eyes to know that I am me.
For you see that without eyes, I still know I have a heart;
I know that I cannot show hate, so I won't even start.
It's okay I'm made this way, GOD made me who I am;
deep inside I know that I am perfect in HIS plan.
It's okay, don't shed a tear, I accept it all;
my heart still beats with love for you; yes, that is why I'm called.
Trusting GOD has been my walk, without legs or even eyes to see;
it's okay, I understand, who others see is me.
They know the way that I was made, for now I compensate;
I've seen although I cannot see, I still can see by faith.
I call things as I see it is by faith that I believe;
that even though I'm made this way, it will not always be.
I know because I believe that one day, I will run;
this life is but a vapor, so I trust in GOD's own SON.
Who died for me and rose again, who won the victory;
yes, it's okay I am this way; HE did it all for me.
In heaven, I will see it all, the beauty yet to be;
I'll run and play; HE'S made a way, for all eternity.
So it's okay for you to see, I'm different.
"It's okay." I still can hear the things you say;
but there will come a day, a time when I will see and run;
my GOD has made a way.
In this world, you will find, the differences that be;

I pray you see the same as I; things change when you believe.
So walk by faith, see with new eyes, and fill your heart with love.
Yes, it's okay to live each day; HIS grace will be enough.

Dedicated to all who know we are the same, all in need of a SAVIOR.

The Battle of the Mind

These many scars within me and those which you can see;
are reminders of the battles, as fierce as they could be,
from an adversary who's always fighting me.
This journey's not been easy; the pain I know is real,
it seemed no one could understand, the ways which I would feel.
The gossip and the pointing, untruths that made me cry,
all those words like daggers, cut deep, I nearly died.
You see we've all experienced, those hurts we can't deny,
we all had our own battles; they are a part of life.
Rejections and abandonment, like drowning in the deep,
letting go of those we loved, those we did not get to keep.
The losses which were hard to bear, our loved ones who had died,
took there tolls and left the scars, that they said would heal in time.
I've learned so much in all these years, as my hair has turned to gray,
the only ONE who's calmed my fears, has never gone away.
HE'S been here from the very start, and has not left my side,
from that moment I believed in HIM, and gave up my foolish pride.
This journey here's not over, and neither is yours, my friend,
don't give up hope, the battle's won, though we have not seen its end.
The grace we have in CHRIST by faith, will surely see us through;
HE is the ONE, the ONLY WAY, and HE will take care of you.
Those battles that I thought were mine, I soon had come to find,
each one had a reason; GOD'S will was done each time.
HE carried me through every storm; it is HE who walks the seas,
each tear I'd cried, HE soon would dry, because HE so loves me.
HE sent HIS SON to save my soul, upon that cursed tree,
I was lost and needed hope; that's where HE first found me.
Broken me upon my knees, dead in all my sin,
HE gave me life for when HE died, that's when my life began.

When I believed in what HE'D done, by faith, I called HIS name,
I still have my struggles, friends, but my life's not been the same.
I've learned and I must understand, that all will change in time,
for in the twinkle of an eye, I'll leave this world behind.
I've also learned this to be true, that we must stand and fight,
that we should love and understand, the battles in our mind.
We wrestle not against flesh and blood, of those who we can see,
there are demonic forces (this too I must believe).
As long as we hold on to GOD, HE is and for eternity will be,
the ONE who sits upon HIS throne, who loves both you and me.
So whatever now will come your way, just know HE'S on your side,
the battle has been won, my friends, this battle in our mind.
HIS WORD is TRUTH and cannot lie; HE is our hope and stay,
learn of HIM, HE is our LIGHT, the ONE the ONLY WAY.

Amazing Grace

Don't point the fingers away from yourself,
you should know you're own sin like nobody else.
Who are we to condemn what others do,
before judging them, first look at you.
GOD's grace is given to all who confess the sin in themselves,
those who see their own mess.
No one is worse, for all sin is the same,
and the wages of sin will one day be paid.
Death and destruction awaits those who deny,
the blood shed for us that was meant to give life.
There is no other name, both in heaven and earth,
that can save us from hell, that can give us new birth.
JESUS, GOD'S SON, who suffered and died,
who on the third day arose back to life.
HE who sits at the FATHER'S right hand even now,
as HE prays for the ones who have chosen to bow.
"FATHER, I'm guilty and in brokenness, cry,
for seeing the speck and not the beam in my eye."
"Forgive me and show me to see as YOU see,
that I to might have grace to those around me."
"That I am quick to forgive as for me YOU have done,
help me to trust as I follow YOUR SON."
"That I may so love the same way as YOU do;
as I hold on by my faith, help me to be true."
"I pray that one day as we meet face to face;
YOU will say, "Well done."
Until then, thank YOU for YOUR amazing grace;
which was given to us by the blood of YOUR SON."

About the Author

I have written poetry since the age of fourteen. I am now a grandfather of fourteen grandchildren and three great-grandchildren, widowed but now reengaged to Beverly, who is a born-again Christian, also widowed with two children. They reside in Manila, Philippines.

My prayer is that this book will encourage and bless all who read it on their own journey home. I am also praying for the success of this book, that GOD receives all glory for the inspiration of its accumulation throughout my journey. HE has brought us this far and will take us home.

After my wife died, I was homeless for four years, have traveled to many states along the way, meeting many wonderful people. I was inspired by those on this journey, by folks who needed a word of encouragement, many homeless themselves, and sharing on the internet. I came to the conclusion that these inspired poems which GOD has put in my heart are not for the many few, but for world in need of the gospel and the love, truth, and encouragement needed in these last days. May those who read these poems find solace in these stressful times and faith in the ONE who has overcome the world.

CPSIA information can be obtained
at www.ICGtesting.com
Printed in the USA
LVHW030030160421
684696LV00008B/275